P9-ASN-046

The Holocaust in Books and Films

A Selected, Annotated List

International Center
for Holocaust Studies,
Anti-Defamation League
of B'nai B'rith

HIPPOCRENE BOOKS, INC.
New York 1986

CO-EDITORS:
JUDITH HERSCHLAG MUFFS is Associate Director of the Inter-
faith Affairs Department, Anti-Defamation League of B'nai
B'rith.
DENNIS B. KLEIN is Director of the International Center for
Holocaust Studies, Anti-Defamation League of
B'nai B'rith.

Third Edition, 1986

The illustrations used in this publication are from
Spiritual Resistance, U.A.H.C. We gratefully acknowledge
the publisher's permission to reproduce them. See the entry
in the text for further information.

Published by Hippocrene Books, 171 Madison Avenue,
New York, NY 10016.

ISBN 0-87052-292-2

For further information write to the:
International Center for Holocaust Studies
Anti-Defamation League of B'nai B'rith
823 United Nations Plaza
New York, NY 10017

Contents

The International Center for Holocaust Studies

Foreword

Until perhaps ten years ago, few beyond a small group of survivors and scholars were willing to mention the crisis that destroyed European Jewish life and a third of world Jewry. In the past decade, however, discussion of the Holocaust has proliferated to a point that has marred the basic effort to record and interpret. As a consequence, ignorance has often given way to indignity and misrepresentation. From its international, historical, and political perspectives, the Anti-Defamation League of B'nai B'rith is accelerating its efforts to help advance and focus the public discussion.

In 1977, the ADL founded the International Center for Holocaust Studies — a public educational resource, and research institute. In addition to evaluating the magnitude of Jewish physical and cultural destruction within a broad historical context, the Center has established a special objective of showing the enduring repercussions of the Holocaust.

Over the past few years, the Center has achieved national distinction in developing and implementing curriculum guides; conducting training workshops and seminars for educators; producing and distributing books, films, exhibits, and special programs for radio and television; sponsoring public conferences, symposia, and literary competitions; publishing *Dimensions, A Journal of Holocaust Studies*; maintaining a comprehensive repository of books and periodicals; and generally serving as a central public resource for the diffusion of accurate and seminal information.

Working closely with ADL's regional offices, the International Center for Holocaust Studies — located in ADL's national office in New York — aims at initiating, implementing, and assisting programs for schools, religious institutions, community groups, and for the general public.

Preface

The Telling of the War
by Elie Wiesel

Somewhere in Europe, on the other side of vast oceans and towering walls, there was, once upon a time, a kingdom of malediction where children were not allowed to live and old men were afraid to be seen. But the children, too, were old. And so, all the inhabitants looked alike. Except that they were divided into two distinct gorups: those who shouted and those who trembled; those who struck and those who were struck down. The killers killed, the victims vanished without leaving a trace, almost without regret. For in this sad and morbid land, people lived and died under the sign of the executioner — he was king and sovereign. And human life was worth less than a speck of dust and weighed less than a handful of ashes. . . For years and years, parents did their best to shield their children from a subject they considered too depressing. Why burden them with the complexes and traumas of the Holocaust? One can understand their point of view; one can almost

share their misgivings. For it is indeed too cruel a subject. What good is it to tell children of man's endless capacity to do evil? To describe to them atrocities that challenge reason as much as faith? They will grow up; they will find out. That was the prevalent attitude of parents. Suddenly the situation has changed. The theme of the Holocaust is no longer taboo. It is now discussed freely — sometimes too freely and too much. Because an entire generation separates our young from the event? Because we have accepted its inextricable ties to Jewish destiny, a destiny doomed to remain in the limelight? The fact is that today (more than ever before) Jews have begun to study this period of torment as depicted by history books and literary documents. Today people even dare speak of the Holocaust to children . . . Young people today don't wish to be shielded. They want to learn about this heinous kingdom where, long ago, the young were not allowed to live — and

neither were the old. They want to
penetrate into the forbidden
orchard where man, robbed of all
masks and illusions, was either victim or executioner; one or the other.
And it is a good omen that parents
. . . have mustered the courage to
speak to them of their own tangled
hopes and anxieties — of their own
childhood and the death of that
childhood.

Elie Wiesel, prolific chronicler of
the Holocaust is chairman of the
United States Holocaust Memorial
Council.

Introduction

Some people have lived with the Holocaust from its beginnings. For others, not only for the young, learning about the Holocaust comes as a shocking revelation. We hope this Resource Guide will assist students, teachers and librarians in their search to find out what happened, to try to understand some of the factors which brought such a cataclysmic event about, to gain a better understanding of the Jewish people, to reflect on their own lives and attitudes, and to resolve that humanity cannot allow a Holocaust to happen again to anyone, anywhere, anytime.

Some notes about this publication and the audience for whom it is intended:
This edition includes approximately 475 entries, some 65 more than in the previous edition. It is not exhaustive, nor is it meant to be. It is designed primarily as a guide for teachers and librarians in the junior and senior high schools. Since several books of a scholarly nature have also been included, the guide will serve university-level courses as well. Some very few publications are addressed to lower elementary grade students.

Reading Levels

Determining the reading level for the various materials is a somewhat arbitrary task, since interest and motivation, more often than not, will be the key to the reader's comprehension. Still, we felt it necessary to give the teacher some broad guidelines to use at his or her discretion. The code is as follows:
   E= grades 4-6
   Where a publication is not only on an elementary reading level but intended for younger students, we have so indicated.
   J= grades 7-9
   S= grades 10-12
   C= college student, teacher, adult
   Almost all of the films listed are suitable for viewing for 8th graders and up.

Books in Print

Although in checking *Books in Print* we found an inordinate number of publications we had included in the last edition to be out of print, we nonetheless decided to keep them for this edition. Books go in and out of print — and in again —with increasing rapidity, and it is not possible to know what the status of a particular book will be by the time this edition is published. In addition, many of those books that are indeed out of print will be available in libraries.

Bibliographic Information

When a book has gone through several publishers, we have given only the most recent hardcover publication data for it. Where there is a different publisher for the paperback edition we have included this information.

Occasionally, because we no longer had access to the publication, the number of pages may be missing. We ask the readers' indulgence for these omissions. The symbol (ADL) indicates the item is available through the ADL.

Categories

Although some publications and films might well have been listed in two or three categories, we have listed them where we felt their primary focus to be. Thus, for example, survivor memoirs which deal primarily with resistance have been placed under "Resistance" and not under "Memoirs." In general, we have not separated fiction and nonfiction. The one exception is "Camps, Ghettos, In Hiding," where the number of items was large enough to warrant separate sections.

Novels and Feature Films on the Holocaust

While often rooted in fact, the function of fiction is to create another dimension in our awareness of the event — the dimension of subjectivity, of heightened sensitivity. These works are not substitutes for works of non-fiction but, when effective, they help bring the reader/viewer into the world of the Holocaust by often focusing on specific issues and problems in a more incisive, human or philosophic manner. Some novels and feature films may contain "inaccuracies" or "distortions." Readers/viewers should try to set their objections aside for the sake of another truth.

Editions of the Guide

The first edition was based on the materials prepared by Roselle Chartock, Ruth Routtenberg Seldin and Dr. Henry Friedlander. Readers were Erika Merems, Great Neck High School, and Deborah Brody, children's book editor at Viking. Readers for the second edition were Erika Merems and Dr. Josephine Knopp, author of "The Trial of Judaism in Contemporary Jewish Writing" (University of Illinois), and former director of the National Holocaust Institute in Philadelphia. We wish to thank them and the many publishers and film distributors, especially the Jewish Lecture Bureau, who provided the materials for our viewing and reading. For the past and present editions, thanks to Theodore Freedman, ADL Director of Intergroup Relations, for his support. For this Third Edition we thank Dr. Marcia Posner, Library Consultant to JWB Jewish Book Council and the New York Federation of Jewish Philanthropies, for her advice; to Stacey Freeman; and to Dr. Dennis B. Klein, Director of the Center, for keeping the project moving.

— J.H.M.

European Jewry Before the Holocaust

The general impression created by the Jewish people in Europe just before the Nazi era was one of extraordinary resourcefulness and vitality in the midst of a great world crisis and an equally severe crisis in Jewish life. . . They were able to develop during the interwar period certain new forms of communal and cultural living which fructified Jewish life throughout the world, contributed significantly to human civilization, and held out great promise for the future. All this was cut short by the Nazi attack.

Salo Baron
From A Historian's Notebook

PUBLICATIONS

Baron, Salo W.
From A Historian's Notebook: European Jewry Before and After Hitler
New York: American Jewish Committee;
54 pp. Paper.

Based on a memorandum the eminent historian prepared for himself when called to testify at the Eichmann Trial in 1961. Deals primarily with European Jewry in the 1930's: demographic changes, economic trends, emancipation, community and intellectual life. Also discusses life under the Nazis and the effects of the Holocaust. SC

Irene Awret, *Young Man in Golf Trousers, Seated, 1943*

Dawidowicz, Lucy S., editor
The Golden Tradition: Jewish Life and Thought in Eastern Europe
New York: Schocken, 1984, 512 pp. Paper.

Anthology of essays of East European Jewish writers, intellectuals, and leaders from late 19th to early 20th century. Excellent 100-page historical overview introduction by the editor. JSC

Dobroszycki, Lucjan and Barbara Kirshenblatt-Gimblett
Image Before My Eyes: A Photographic History of Jewish Life in Poland, 1864–1939
New York: Schocken, 1977, 242 pp. Paper. (ADL)

Polish Jewry, once the largest Jewish community in Europe, a world center of Jewish cultural creativity, no longer exists. This album of three hundred photographs selected from over 10,000 housed at the YIVO Institute for Jewish Research gives us an eyewitness pictorial account of all aspects of Polish Jewish life. Beautiful, revealing, moving. For library acquisition. EJSC

Grunfeld, Frederic V.
Prophets Without Honor: A Background to Freud, Kafka, Einstein and Their World
New York: McGraw-Hill, 1980, 347 pp. Paper.

The lives, the works and the ideals of a constellation of German-speaking Jews –scientists, writers, artists – during the first three decades of the 20th Century, set against the current of German politics, society and culture. "An intellectual adventure," Lucy Dawidowicz. SC

Heller, Celia S.
On the Edge of Destruction: Jews of Poland Between the Two World Wars
New York: Schocken, 1980, 384 pp. Paper.

The author, a sociologist, describes the attempt of Jews to deal with the fierce anti-Semitism ushered in with Polish independence in 1918. The overwhelming majority of almost 3 million Polish Jews were Orthodox traditional, but there was a growing number of Jewish nationalists (Zionists and Jewish socialists), Bundists, and a small group of assimilationists. Acculturation and secularization did not diminish anti-Semitism or the rigid caste line dividing Poles and Jews. Two vital aspects of understanding Jews in this period relate to secularization and the increasing internal differentiation within the Jewish population. An important study. C

Heschel, Abraham J.
The Earth is the Lord's: The Inner World of the Jew in East Europe
New York: Farrar, Straus & Giroux, 1978, 109 pp. Paper.

A magnificent evocation of the soul

and spirit of a world that is no more — the daily life, habits and customs, attitudes and scale of values which governed the aspirations of the Jews of Eastern Europe. JSC

Howe, Irving and Eliezer Greenberg, editors
A Treasury of Yiddish Stories
New York: Schocken, 1973, 630 pp. Paper.

Wide-ranging collection from works by Sholom Aleichem to Saul Bellow's translation of Isaac Bashevis Singer's "Gimpel the Fool." Contains a lengthy analytical introduction on Yiddish literature. SC

Howe, Irving and Eliezer Greenberg, editors
Voices from the Yiddish: Essays, Memoirs, & Diaries
New York: Schocken, 1975, 340 pp. Paper.

Yiddish writings over 80 years, originally intended for an "internal" audience. From a sociological investigation of the shtetl to a survey of modernistic influences of yiddish poetry in America; memoirs of life in New York in the 1880's to memoirs of a Holocaust survivor. SC

Kugelmass, Jack and Jonathan Boyarin
From a Ruined Garden: The Memorial Books of Polish Jewry
New York: Schocken, 1983, 275 pp. Also paper.

A beautiful and loving collection gleaned from over 100 community memorial books written by survivors. Most of the book deals with life before the Holocaust. It brings us the multifaceted life of the Jewish communities of Otvosk, Nowogrodek, Belchatow et al., their politics, their religion, their local characters, and finally, their destruction. At the end of the book there is a 41-page bibliography of Eastern European Memorial books. It can be the basis of an important lesson in the geography of the Holocaust. Highly recommended. JSC

Aizik Feder, *Portrait of a Man with a Yellow Star, Reading, 1942-1943*

Meltzer, Milton
World of Our Fathers:
The Jews
of Eastern Europe
New York: Farrar, Straus &
Giroux, 1974, xiii, 256 pp.

A picture of East European Jews up
to World War I, simply written.
Incorporates excerpts from eyewitness accounts, diaries, songs, etc.
Illustrated. EJS

Noren, Catherine Hanf
The Camera
of My Family
New York: Knopf, 1976, 239 pp.

Photographs and mementos of 5
generations of a German-Jewish
family, from their lives in Germany
before the turn of the century to the
American present. See filmstrip
below. EJSC.

Poppel, Stephen M.
Zionism in Germany 1897-1933:
The Shaping of a Jewish Identity
Philadelphia: Jewish Publication
Society, 1977,
234 pp.

Set against a background of Jewish
and German history this work shows
how Zionist ideology operated to
shape a new Jewish identity within
Germany, paradoxically making German Zionists all the more comfortable in remaining where they were.
SC

Charlotte Buresova, Deportation, the
Last Road, c. 1944

Roskies, Diane K. and David G.
The Shtetl Book
New York: ADL and KTAV, 1975, xiii
and 327 pp. Paper.

A book about real people, places
and events – Yiddish-speaking Jews
in villages (shtetls) in Eastern
Europe 1800-1914 – their stories,
songs, history, problems. Heavy use
of primary sources, illustrations.
EJSC

Singer, Isaac Bashevis
A Day of Pleasure: Stories of a
Boy Growing Up in Warsaw
New York: Farrar, Straus & Giroux,
1969. Also paper.

The Nobel laureate recounts his
childhood in the first decades of
this century. Wonderful. EJSC

Singer, Isaac Bashevis
In My Father's Court
New York: Farrar, Straus & Giroux,
1966, 307 pp. Also paper. Fawcett,
1979. Paper.

The Nobel laureate reminisces
about growing up in Warsaw. His
father was an impoverished rabbi
whose congregants often called on
him to decide ritual, personal and
civil issues. JSC

Vishniac, Roman
Polish Jews: A Pictorial Record
Introduction by Abraham
Joshua Heschel.
New York: Schocken, 1968.
Also Paper.
Classic collection of photographs taken on the eve of World War II. EJSC

Zborowski, Mark and Elizabeth Herzog
Life is with People: The Culture of the Shtetl
New York: Schocken, 1962, 452 pp. Paper.
Anthropologists' very readable composite of life of Jews in small communities in Eastern Europe before World War II. Classic. JSC

Zweig, Stefan
The World of Yesterday: An Autobiography
Introduction by Harry Zohn.
Darby, PA: Arden Library, 1977; University of Nebraska Press, 1964, xxiii + 455 pp. Paper.
Mirrors three ages. The "world of security" before World War I, the turbulent, fruitful period following it and the Hitler era to the beginning of World War II. A distinguished novelist, biographer, dramatist, he called himself "an Austrian, a Jew, an author, a humanist, and a pacifist." His religion was Europe. He watched it commit suicide and then took his own life. C

AUDIO-VISUAL

Image Before My Eyes
90 minutes/black and white/Cinema Five
Made by Josh Waletzky for YIVO and consisting chiefly of old home movies, photographs and interviews with emigres and refugees, this film succeeds in giving the reviewer a multifaceted picture of Jewish life in Poland before the war. Though the religious aspects are somewhat minimized, scenes are from Korczak's school, from "show biz," town markets with peddlers and beggars, the current of German politics, society and culture. "An intellectual adventure," Lucy Dawidowicz. SC

The Third Reich

Bismarck's unique creation is the Germany we have known in our time . . . in which first this remarkable man and then Kaiser Wilhelm II and finally Hitler, aided by a military caste . . . succeeded in inculcating a lust for power and domination, a passion for unbridled militarism, a contempt for democracy and individual freedom and a longing for authority.

William L. Shirer

PUBLICATIONS

Allen, William Sheridan
The Nazi Seizure of Power: The Experience of a Single German Town 1922-1945
Second Revised Edition.
New York: Franklin Watts, 1984, 416 pp.
Also paper. (ADL, paper)

Using interviews and contemporary records, the author, a professor of history at SUNY, analyzes the activism of the Nazis, the strengths and weaknesses of the Social Democrats, the attitudes of the nationalistic middle class, voting trends, the growth of political activity and partisan violence, etc.
SC

Blackburn, Gilmer W.
Education in the Third Reich: Race and History in Nazi Textbooks
Albany, NY: SUNY Press, 1984, 217 pp.

The author examined textbooks from every level plus theoretical works by educational officials and writings of Nazi political leaders. His findings: The central theme was to arouse in the student a sense of Germanism in accordance with the most exclusive definition which would kindle the urgent desire to secure Germany's permanent hegemony in the world. Nazi history was apocalyptic in that it embodied meaning and mission. For the student, neither detachment nor interpretation was allowed, nor were questions left unanswered. The author speaks of the adolescent nature of National Socialism and how this facilitated its acceptance by adolescents of its historical writings. Interesting for all — but especially for teachers of history. C

Brecht, Bertolt
The Jewish Wife and Other Short Plays
Translated from the German by Eric Bentley. New York: Grove, 1965, 174 pp. Paper.

Six plays related to this period, by a leading German anti-Nazi playwright. (See film below.) JSC

Bridenthal, Renata, et al., ed.
When Biology Became Destiny: Women in Weimar and Nazi Germany
New York: Monthly Review Press, 1984, 416 pp. Cloth, Paper.

A collection of essays and criticism about the "outsider" phenomenon in Weimar and Nazi Germany. Particularly relevant are two articles: "Sisterhood under Siege: Feminism and Anti-Semitism in Germany, 1904-1938," by Marion Kaplan and "Women and the Holocaust: The Case of German and German-Jewish Women" by Sybil Milton. C

Browning, Christopher R.
Fateful Months: Essays on the Emergence of the Final Solution
New York: Holmes and Meier, 1985, 87pp. Cloth.

In four related essays, Browning shows that what was happening to the Jews in the Nazi-occupied territories affected the political decisions being made about them in Berlin. To explain the roots of the "Final Solution," Browning takes into account Hitler's strong intention to annihilate the Jews as well as the impact of local problems on middle and lower-echelon administrators, who had the practical responsibility for the Jews in the occupied territories. C

Bullock, Alan
Hitler: A Study in Tyranny
New York: Harper & Row, 1964, 776 pp. Torchbook. Paper.

The standard scholarly biography: Hitler as party leader, chancellor and warlord. C

Conway, John S.
The Nazi Persecution of the Churches, 1933-45
New York: Basic Books, 1968, xxxi+474 pp

Comprehensive and scholarly treatment of Nazi policy vis-a-vis the German Protestant and Catholic churches and of their reaction. Covers both persecution and compliance. C

Fest, Joachim C.
The Face of the Third Reich: Portraits of the Nazi Leadership
Translated from the German by Michael Bullock. New York: Pantheon, 1977, 402 pp. Paper.

Eighteen well-written sketches of Hitler and the "practitioners, functionaries and technicians of totalitarian rule." According to the author, "the National Socialist leaders were fundamentally nothing more than particularly well marked examples of a type that was to be met throughout society and in this sense the face of the Third Reich was the face of a whole nation." SC

Forman, James
The Traitors
New York: Farrar, Straus & Giroux, 1968, 238pp.

Novel about two half-brothers. One becomes a Nazi, the other helps their father who is a pastor, in trying to save a Jewish friend. Well written. JS

Gordon, Sarah
Hitler, Germans and the "Jewish Question"
Princeton, N.J.: Princeton University Press, 1984, 416pp. Paper.

Nominated for the National Jewish Book Award, this book probes the character of anti-Semitism in Nazi Germany and the German people's reaction to the National Socialist reign of terror. Gordon depicts the emergence in Weimar Germany of a new kind of extreme anti-Semite, of which Hitler was the paramount example. Drawing on hitherto unexamined documentary sources, she also answers some frequently asked questions: To what extent did the German people know about Hitler's intentions and actions? How many opposed Nazi anti-Semitism, and who aided the Jews or publicly criticized their persecution? Some of the answers are disturbing. C

Grunberger, Richard
Twelve Year Reich: A Social History of Nazi Germany 1933-45
New York: Holt, Rinehart & Winston, 1979, vi+535 pp. Paper.

Narrative covering education, sports, the arts, family life, Nazi speech, humor, etc. Based on original contemporary materials. Illustrated. SC

Otto Karas-Kaufman, *The Living Block, L 205, 1943*

Grunfeld, Frederic V.
The Hitler File: A Social History of Germany and the Nazis, 1918-45
New York: Random House, 1974, 374 pp.

Essentially a pictorial review — over 750 black-and-white illustrations, 48 pages of color illustrations. Posters, cartoons, photos, art. Expecially helpful for non-readers. EJSC

Halperin, Samuel W.
Germany Tried Democracy
New York: Cromwell, 1946, 567 pp.; Norton 1965; Ann Arbor: Xerox University of Michigan Microfilm.

A political history of the Reich from 1917-1933. Standard work. C

Heartfield, John
Photomontages of the Nazi Period
New York: Universe Books, 1977, 143 pp. Paper.

Heartfield was a German Dadaist, a communist and gifted artist. His biting anti-Nazi works appeared in German periodicals through the 1930's. More than 90 illustrations. EJSC

Hillel, Marc and Clarissa Henry
Of Pure Blood
New York: McGraw-Hill, 1977, 256pp.

The authors spent three years tracking down the sources about the Lebensborn (Fountain of Life) organization, which kidnapped "racially valuable" children from Germany and all over Europe, "Germanized" them and used them for breeding a "master race." Over 200,000 were taken from Poland alone. The shocking story of the breeders and their offspring is dramatically told. JSC

Hinz, Berthold
Art in the Third Reich
Translated from the German by Robert and Rita Kimber. New York: Pantheon Books, 1979, 271 pp. Also paper.

From 1933 to 1937 visual artists were given time to adjust to the cultural policy of the new government. During this same period a campaign was mounted against "degenerate" (modern) art and artists. In 1937 the period of art in the Third Reich begins. This is a study of what it meant in terms of the philosophy and psychology of the Third Reich. Deals with paintings, photography and architecture. A serious and interesting compilation. C

Isherwood, Christopher
The Berlin Stories
Cambridge: Robert Bentley, 1979 reprint of 1946 edition; New Directions, 1954. Paper.

A collection of stories, some of them published in the 1930's, which show the decline of German social and cultural life in the 1920's and presage the horrors of Nazism. The film *Cabaret* (see below) was based on this book. SC

Katz, William Loren
An Album of Nazism
New York: Franklin Watts, 1979, 90 pp. (oversize)

Written simply and succinctly with dozens of photographs. Includes comments on the contemporary situation. EJ

Koehn, Ilse
Mischling, Second Degree: My Childhood in Nazi Germany
New York: Greenwillow/William Morrow, 1977, 240 pp.

Ilse Koehn's account of her adolescence in Nazi Germany universalizes the experience of young people bewildered, uprooted and traumatized by war. Her story has an ironic twist, in that under the 1935 Nuremberg Laws she was a "mischling," the "mixed" offspring of a union between a German and Jew, a fact she remained ignorant of until after the war. JS

Lane, Barbara Miller and Leila J. Rupp, editors and translators
Nazi Ideology Before 1933: A Documentation
Austin: University of Texas, 1978, 208 pp.

Political writings of Eckart, Rosenberg, Goebbels, Himmler, Strasser and Darre before the National Socialists came to power. In their introduction Lane and Rupp conclude that before 1933 Nazi ideology was not a consistent whole but a developing doctrine. 28 documents, prefatory notes. C

Mayer, Milton
They Thought They Were Free: The Germans 1933-45
Second edition. Chicago: University of Chicago Press, 1966, 354 pp. Paper.

The author portrays the rise of Nazism as seen through the eyes of ten ordinary citizens in a small German city. For them, the Third Reich meant full employment and a sense of belonging. JSC

Mosse, George L.
The Crisis of German Ideology: Intellectual Origins of the Third Reich
New York: Grosset & Dunlap (Universal Library paperback), 1964, 373 pp. (ADL, paper)

The author is a leading scholar of the history of modern Germany. A comprehensive survey of the ideological roots of Nazism tracing its growth from the early nineteenth century, with special emphasis on education and the youth movement. See in particular chap. 7, "The Jews," and chap. 17, "The Anti-Jewish Revolution." C

Mosse, George L.
The Nationalization of the Masses: Political Symbolism and Mass Movements in Germany from the Napoleonic Wars through the Third Reich
New York: Howard Fertig, 1975, xiv+272 pp.

An authority on modern German history analyzes the esthetics of politics, the role of the theater, gymnast groups, music and public festivals in creating the climate for Nazism, and the seeming need of large numbers of people for a totality of life where all forms of life become politicized. SC

Amalie Seckbach, *Young Internee with Flowers, Seen in a Dream as a Queen, 1943*

Mosse, George L., *editor*
Nazi Culture: Intellectual, Cultural and Social Life in the Third Reich
New York: Schocken, 1981, 432 pp. Paper. (ADL)

Twenty-three page general introduction with full introductions to each section and selection. An anthology — a Nazi children's prayer; a section of a novel by Goebbels; a children's story picturing Hitler as the friend of the young; the Gestapo and the case of a pro-Jewish Christian minister; Hitler speaks against the equal status of women. Illustrated. JSC

Orlow, Dietrich
The History of the Nazi Party: 1919-1933 (Vol. I); 1933-1945 (Vol. II)
Pittsburgh: University of Pittsburgh Press, Vol. I, 1969, 388 pp.; Vol. II, 1973, 538 pp.

Volume I deals with the organizational and administrative history of the German Nazi party in the years of its rise to political power, analyzing the internal development of a totalitarian political party in the context of a pluralistic society (the Weimar Republic). Volume II focuses on the impact of the internal mechanism of the Nazi party in obtaining governmental power and managing foreign conquest. C

Raab, Earl
The Anatomy of Nazism
New York: ADL, 1961, 40 pp. Paper.

Basic description of the components of Nazism — brief historical background, life under Nazism, Nazi philosophy and techniques. 20 pages of illustrations. Conceptually basic, except for Chapter V. "Totalitarianism and Democracy" may be difficult for ninth and/or tenth grade students who have not been exposed to political ideologies. JS

Richter, Hans Peter
I Was There
Translated from German by Edite Kroll.
New York: Holt, Rinehart & Winston, 1972, 224 pp.

The Nazi youth movement and daily living in Germany. "I believed —and I will never believe again." JS

Shirer, William L.
The Rise and Fall of the Third Reich: A History of Nazi Germany
New York: Touchstone (Simon & Schuster), 1981, 1599 pp. Paper.

Massive, well-written, moving and classic account by a noted

American author who lived and worked in Germany in the 1930's. SC

Snyder, Louis L.
The Encyclopedia of the Third Reich
New York: McGraw Hill, 1976, 416 pp.

Handy reference for all facets of the period. JSC.

Snyder, Louis L.
Hitler's Third Reich: A Documentary History
Chicago: Nelson-Hall, 1981, 637 pp.

A noted scholar of German history brings us an account of the Third Reich through a rich variety of original documents — official publications, reportage, speeches, excerpts from diaries and letters, radio talks and court records. The period covered includes the post-World War I years and the Weimar Republic through the rise of Nazism, the Third Reich and Germany immediately after World War II. Snyder provides connective material to place each selection in its historical context. Excellent for classroom use and for everyone's browsing. JSC

Snyder, Louis L.
Hitler and Nazism
New York: Bantam Books, 1967, 182 pp. Paper.

A biography of Hitler and a brief history of the main happenings under the Third Reich. Told very simply, in short, vivid and dramatic chapters. Particularly useful for students who are not likely to read anything more demanding. JS

Switzer, Ellen
How Democracy Failed
New York: Atheneum, 1975, 169pp.

Excellent book by a German-born writer who went back to interview people her own age. They evoke their teenage years under Nazism and the effect it had on their families and on their own lives. Good, personalized reinforcement of the history of the period. 24 pp. of photographs. JS

Toland, John
Adolf Hitler
New York: Ballantine, 1981, 1056 pp. Paper.

An impressive work of military, social and political history as well as biography, this is a complex and comprehensive portrait of Hitler based on extensive research that draws on a number of previously unavailable sources and interviews with people directly involved in the Fuehrer's private and public life. C

Vogt, Hannah
Burden of Guilt: A Short History of Germany 1914-1945
Translated from the German by H. Strauss. New York: Oxford University Press, 1964. 318 pp. Paper.

A text directed to high school students in Germany today. Hides none of the horrors, exhorts the students to face the reality of the past and accept responsibility for the future. S

Von der Grun, Max
Howl Like the Wolves: Growing Up in Nazi Germany
Translated from the German by Jan Van Heurck. Documentation by Christel Schutz. New York: William Morrow, 1980. 228 pp.

Interweaving of memoirs, history and documents. The author was brought up in an anti-Nazi family but taught by his mother "to howl like the wolves so as not to be eaten by them." Pays much attention to the plight of the Jews. Simply written. JSC

Waite, Robert G., editor
Hitler and Nazi Germany
New York: Holt, Rinehart & Winston, 1969, 122 pp. Paper.

Series of articles and documents. C

AUDIO-VISUAL

The Anatomy of Nazism
55 frames/color with captions

An historic presentation of social, cultural, economic and political workings of Fascism in Hitler's Germany. Although focused on Germany, this filmstrip succeeds in reflecting the general threat to democracy of all forms of totalitarianism. JS

Black Fox
89 minutes/black-and-white/Audio Brandon

Documentary on Hitler using the allegory of the Black Fox by Goethe. Extensive use of art. Narrated by Marlene Dietrich. Considerable time spent on the war, using much footage not seen elsewhere. The Jewish component is minimal, and often the Jewish victims of Nazi atrocities are not identified as such. Nonetheless, especially for a class which is not studying World War II, the film presents background on the rise of the Third Reich and the role of the Allies. JSC

Cabaret
123 minutes/color/feature film/ Allied Artists

Life and decadence in Berlin just prior to the rise of Hitler, based on Christopher Isherwood's *The Berlin Stories* (see above). JSC

From Kaiser to Fuehrer
26 minutes/black-and-white/ McGraw-Hill

The story of the ill-fated Weimar Republic, set up by forward-looking Germans after World War I, and liquidated in 1933 by the combination of economic depression, the inexperience of the Germans at democracy and the doubts of many of its adherents. CBS-TV (20th Century Series). JSC

Hitler's Executioners
78 minutes/black-and-white/Audio Brandon

Utilizing official war records and newsreel clips, this documentary gives an on-the-spot picture report of the rise and fall of Hitler's Third Reich, including his rise to power, promises, the Nazi war machine, and finally the Nuremberg Trials. JSC.

Max van Dam, *Premonition of Death, 1941*

The Making of the German Nation: 1815-1945

4 filmstrips/color/2 records/ cassettes; manual/automatic/ teacher's notes/Educational AudioVisual

Part I deals with German history from 1815 to 1871; Part II: from 1871 to 1918; Part III: from 1918 to 1933; Part IV: from 1933 to 1945.

Mein Kampf

119 minutes/black-and-white/Audio Brandon

A documentary depiction of the modern world's Third Reich. Through the Nazis' own speeches and cameras we see the history of Hitler's rise and his murder machine. Also includes material on his youth and development through World War I. JSC.

Bruno Simon, *Hitler, undated*

Minister of Hate

27 minutes/black-and-white/ McGraw-Hill

Joseph Goebbels, Minister of Propaganda for the Third Reich, controlled the nation's radio, movies, press and theater, orchestrated parades and happenings — all to manipulate and control the mind of the nation. Documented with historical motion picture footage. Narrated by Walter Cronkite. JSC

The Rise and Fall of Nazi Germany

40 photographs/Social Studies School Services

The life of Hitler and the activities of his Third Reich; pictures include early photographs of Hitler, the early days of the Nazi Party, officials, propaganda posters, anti-Semitic activities, rearmament, World War II, parades, celebrations and speeches, and foreign officials, including Stalin, Chamberlain, Franco and Mussolini. Printed on 11"×14" heavy glossy stock.

The Rise and Fall of the Third Reich
A Four-Part Film Series on Nazi Germany
Part I. Rise of Hitler

28 minutes/black-and-white/ADL

With Germany's defeat in World War I, the country faced economic ruin and civil war. The film chronicles how Adolf Hitler and his political cohorts in the Nazi party manipulated events during their country's crises to achieve power: their promulgation of the myth of the Aryan race gave Germans an outlet for their hate and frustration; the Nazis forced a political crisis to overthrow the democratic Weimar Republic; and Hitler emerged as the Chancellor of the Third Reich. JSC

Part II.
Nazi Germany: Years of Triumph
28 minutes/black-and-white/ADL

Germany between 1933 and 1939, when some sixty-seven million people willingly permitted themselves to become puppets of the Third Reich. A silent majority witnessed the collapse of a democratic society, all dissent was squashed, the military became subservient to a "master plan" of world conquest, and the passage of the Nuremberg Laws set the stage for the eventual slaughter of six million Jews. Remarkably, there was little resistance to Hitler until he invaded Poland. JSC

Part III.
Gotterdammerung:
Collapse of the Third Reich
28 minutes/black-and-white/ADL

In the four years between 1941 and 1945, Hitler's dream of a "thousand year Reich" turned into the nightmare of World War II as the free nations of the world joined together to defeat Nazi tyranny. By the spring of 1945, the Allies were victorious. Hitler was dead. JSC

Part IV. Nuremberg Trial
31 minutes/black-and-white/ADL

The indictment of twenty-four Nazi leaders in Nuremberg, Germany, in October 1945, opened an unprecedented chapter in international law. The film traces the trial as it attempted to establish that those who conspire to wage war stand guilty of crimes against humanity. The proceedings lasted for eight months. JSC

Ship of Fools
150 minutes/black-and-white/
Columbia/feature film

Based on the book by Katherine Anne Porter (Signet, 1963). A German luxury oceanliner in the 1930's, with a cross-section of types — Nazis, anti-Nazis, Jews, Americans, optimists, pessimists, innocents and Michael Dunn as the "jester" dwarf. JSC

Triumph of the Will
120 minutes,
abridged version — 50 minutes
black-and-white/Images

The now-famous propaganda film, made for the Third Reich by Leni Riefenstahl, of the 1934 Nazi Party rally held in Nuremberg. An effective document for learning about

Hitler's image of himself, his manipulation of the crowds and his use of film as a propaganda tool. SC

The Twisted Cross
55 minutes/black-and-white/
McGraw-Hill Educational Films

An overview of Hitler's rise to power, the triumphant 1930's and World War II. Good for propaganda study as well as introduction to Nazism. JSC

Jews in the Third Reich

Publications

Appelfeld, Aharon
Badenheim 1939
Translated from the Hebrew by Dalya Bilu.
Boston: David R. Godine, 1980, 144 pp.; G.K. Hall, 1981 (large print).

"By the time you experience the stunning conclusion [of this novel] you understand it is not just the summer of 1939 he is trying to dramatize, but the entire pre-World War II experience of the Jews of Germany and Austria ... Compared with the hidden enemy who haunts the pages of Badenheim 1939, Death and Storm Troopers are nothing." (*New York Times*). From ages 8 to 11, the author, a survivor, wandered in the forests and fields of Eastern Europe. SC

Baer, Edith
A Frost in the Night: A Childhood on the Eve of the Third Reich
New York: Pantheon, 1980, 224 pp.

Autobiographical novel about a family that believed it could be both Jewish and German. Slow-moving. EJ

Baker, Leonard
Days of Sorrow and Pain: Leo Baeck and the Berlin Jews
New York: Oxford University Press, 1980, 412 pp. Paper.

Explores the disintegration of German society and the philosophy of Rabbi Baeck by which he guided the Jews of Germany during the Nazi period. Baeck was later sent to Theresienstadt. Difficult. Pulitzer Prize winner. C

Kolmar, Gertrud
Dark Soliloquy: The Selected Poems of Gertrud Kolmar
Translated from the German by Henry A. Smith.
New York: Seabury, 1975, 261 pp.

Achieving some recognition before Kristallnacht (Night of Broken Glass) in 1938, the author was sentenced as a poet and a Jew, to forced labor and finally death at Auschwitz in 1943 at age 48. Her poems deal with the image of women, nature and the world. In German with English translations, and a 50-page introduction on the poet's life and works by Henry A. Smith. (See also Grunfeld, *Prophets Without Honor*.) SC

Laqueur, Walter
The Missing Years
Boston: Little, Brown, 1980, 281 pp.

An eminent historian of the 20th century (*Weimer: A Cultural History; A History of Zionism: Terrorism*) turns to fiction to tell the story of a German Jewish doctor, his "Aryan" wife and their two children who remained in Germany under the Nazi regime. Based on fact. SC

Orgel, Doris
The Devil in Vienna
New York: Dial Press, 1978, 246 pp.

Novel based on the author's experience in Vienna, 1938. Inga is Jewish. Liselotte, at the insistence of her Nazi father, is in the Hitler Youth movement. The girls are thirteen years old and blood-sisters. Set against the background of the *Anschluss*, when the situation of the Jews became more and more desperate. A good story. EJ

Richter, Hans Peter
Friedrich
Translated from the German by Edite Kroll.
New York: Dell, 1973, 157 pp.

Novel about a German boy and his friendship with a Jewish boy, Friedrich, during the years of Nazism. Useful chronology adds to student's understanding. Excellent for all levels. Conceptually basic. EJS

Thalmann, Rita and Emmanuel Feinermann
Crystal Night: 9-10 November 1938
Translated from the French by Gilles Cremonesi.
New York: Holocaust Library, 1980, 192 pp. Also paper.
(ADL, paper)

An account of the events surrounding the rioting which led to the destruction of all the synagogues in Germany, terrorization, looting and the imprisonment of thousands of Jews. Based on authenticated documents and testimonies. Illustrated. JSC

Uhlman, Fred
Reunion
New York: Farrar, Straus & Giroux,
1977, 112 pp.; Penguin, 1978.
Paper.

Novella about two schoolboys in
Germany in the early 1930's — one
the son of a Jewish doctor, the
other a German aristrocrat. JCS

AUDIO-VISUAL

The Camera of My Family
123 frames/18½ minutes/color and
black-and-white/cassette or tape/
ADL

Catherine Hanf Noren came to this
country as a six-year-old refugee
from Germany. The discovery of her
grandparents' collection of family
photographs motivated her search
for knowledge about her upper-
middle class family who had lived
in Germany for more than two hundred years and their fate during the
Nazi period. Winner of several
awards. Student guide available.
(See book in above.) JSC

The Jewish Wife
28 minutes/color/feature film/Alden

Based on the one-act play by Bertolt Brecht. A Jewish woman
decides she must leave her "Aryan"
husband and flee the country. Moving performance by Viveca Lindfors.
(See play in above.) SC

Marriage in the Shadows
96 minutes/black-and-white/feature
film/Audio Brandon/JWB Lecture
Bureau/German with English titles.

Based on a true story of a mixed
marriage in Nazi Germany, the film
attacks those — especially artists
— who actively or passively went
along with the Nazis. SC

We Were German Jews: The
Story of Herbert and Lotte
Strauss
58 minutes/color/Blackwood

A portrait of German Jewry during
the Third Reich, recounted by Herbert and Lotte Strauss. (He is now
a professor of history at City
College, New York.) They tell of the
fate of their families and friends, of
their own dramatic escape from the
Gestapo, and of their adjustment to
a new life in a new country. Raises
serious questions about "German-
Jewish Mentality" during the Nazi
period. SC

Holocaust Overview

The missionaries of Christianity had said in effect: You have no right to live among us as Jews. The secular rulers who followed, had proclaimed: You have no right to live among us. The German Nazis at last decreed: You have no right to live.

Raul Hilberg
The Destruction of
the European Jews

PUBLICATIONS

Histories

Altshuler, David A.
Hitler's War Against the Jews.
New York: Behrman House, 1978, 190 pp. Also paper. (ADL paper)

Adapted for young readers from *The War Against the Jews, 1933-1945* and *A Holocaust Reader* by Lucy S. Dawidowicz. Includes 100 photographs and original source readings. EJS

Bauer, Yehuda
A History of the Holocaust
New York: Franklin Watts, 1982, 416 pp. Paper.

Set against a background of Jewish-Gentile relationships, a summary of Jewish history and the roots of anti-Semitism. The author explores human resistance as a prelude to dealing with armed resistance. He reviews the

Holocaust years in detail, country by country. Glossary, bibliography, index. Well written. Excellent for high school level textbook. JSC

Dawidowicz, Lucy S.
The War Against The Jews, 1933-1945
New York: Bantam, 1976, 640 pp. Paper.

An account of the Holocaust as it completed the Nazi vision and as it affected the Jews of Eastern Europe. It is the author's contention that anti-Semitism was the core of Hitler's system of beliefs and the central motivation for his policies. Part II, "The Holocaust," dealing with Jewish reactions, is especially recommended. JSC

Gilbert, Martin
Atlas of the Holocaust
London, Eng.: Michael Joseph,
1982, 256 pp., also paper. (ADL
paper)

Three hundred and sixteen (316)
maps and 45 photos plus historical
commentary. Examples: The Jews
of Macedonia and Thrace deported
March 3-22, 1943; German
euthanasia centers, 1940; Anti-
Jewish violence and Jewish self-
defense in Poland, 1935-47; Gypsy
deportations, massacres and revolt,
1939-45; and Children under four
deported (from France) to
Auschwitz, August 17, 1942.
Excellent teaching tool. EJSC

Gilbert, Martin
**Final Journey: The Fate of the
Jews in Nazi Europe**
New York: Mayflower Books, 1979,
224 pp.

The book is essentially a weaving
together of eyewitness accounts
and contemporary evidence. There
is an abundance of photographs
and maps plus a highly useful
index. Minor note: The typesetting
makes the reading somewhat difficult. Illustrated. JSC

Hilberg, Raul
**The Destruction of
the European Jews**
Revised edition.
New York: Holmes & Meier, 1985,
1000 pp. Also paper.

This is a landmark new edition of

the classic work that established
the author in the early 1960's as
the leading American scholar of the
Holocaust. The product of more
than twenty additional years of
research. This massive work
describes in minute detail the
conception and execution of the
Nazi program of extermination,
adding a convincing and per-
ceptive analysis. The strength and
bulk of the work stem from the
meticulous presentation of the destructive process (pp. 43-638).
Hilberg focuses on the perpetrators,
not on the victims. "Insofar as we
may examine Jewish institutions we
will do so primarily through the
eyes of the Germans; as tools
which were used in the destructive
process." The introductory section –
precedents, antecedents, scope and
organization – and the conclusion –
reflections, consequences and
implications – should not be
ignored. Indispensable. SC

Hilberg, Raul
**The Destruction of the
European Jews**
New York: Holmes and Meier,
1985, 350 pp. Paper (Student
Edition).

This student edition is an
abridgement of Hilberg's definitive
three-volume study. The book
focuses on the machinery of destruction and the bureaucratic network that set the machinery in
motion and sheds new light on

many important aspects of the Holocaust.
SC

Levin, Nora
The Holocaust: The Destruction of European Jewry, 1933-1945
New York: Schocken, 1973,
784 pp. Paper. (ADL)

Popular history, well written. Attempts to write "from the inside" emphasizing the "failures" of German Jewry, the "dilemmas" of the Jewish Councils, and resistance. JSC

Holocaust
Jerusalem: Keter, 1974,
214 pp. Paper.

Compiled from material originally published in the *Encyclopedia Judaica* (Macmillan). Sections on history, behavior of the victims, the camps, Hitler, partisans, rescue, Christian churches, war crimes, Eichmann trial, historiography. SC

✓ *Meltzer, Milton*
Never to Forget: The Jews of the Holocaust
New York: Harper & Row, 1976,
xvi + 217 pp.; Dell, 1977,
192 pp. Paper. (ADL paper)

Exceptionally well-written account of the roots of German anti-Semitism, Hitler's rise to power, the workings of the Nazi death machine, life in the ghettos and camps, the resis-

tance movement, and other aspects of the subject. Includes excerpts from private letters. Dell has Teacher's Guide by Max Nadel. EJS

Poliakov, Leon
Harvest of Hate:
The Nazi Program for the Destruction of the Jews in Europe
Translated from the French. Revised and expanded edition. Foreword by Reinhold Niebuhr.
New York: Holocaust Library, 1979,
350 pp. Paper. (ADL, paper)

Brief, concise, with extensive quotes from the original sources. Includes a chapter on Nazi plans for "inferior peoples." SC

The Record:
The Holocaust in History 1933-1945
New York: ADL-NCS, 1985 (revised),
16 pp.

Newspaper format using articles from newspapers of the period and archive photographs. Includes discussion and study guides and glossary. EJS

Reitlinger, Gerald
The Final Solution:
The Attempt to Exterminate the Jews of Europe, 1939-1945
2nd revised and augmented edition. New York: Barnes, 1961,
xii + 668 pp. Paper.

The course of events of the Final Solution reconstructed from the secret files of the Third Reich. The first comprehensive history. Includes: Forced Emigration and Pogroms before September, 1939; Deportations, 1939-41; the Ghettos 1940-42; Madagascar Project and Deportations to Lodz and Russia; Wannsee Conference and the Auschwitz Plan; the Gas Chambers; Fate of the Reich Jews and the Fight for Exemption. Country by country. Maps, chronology. SC

Rossel, Seymour
The Holocaust
New York: Franklin Watts, 1981, 148 pp.

An historical account with emphasis on the universal issues involved: passive and active resistance to evil; justice and injustice; and the moral responsibility of governments. EJS

Rubin, Arnold P.
The Evil That Men Do: The Story of the Nazis
New York: Julian Messner, 1981, 224 pp.

People in Germany and all over the world were faced with choices that had to be made. This book talks about the circumstances leading up to those choices and about the people involved – Jewish and non-Jewish victims, concentration camp inmates, clergy, children and citizens around the world. Told simply and with passion. EJ

Schoenberner, Gerhard
The Yellow Star: The Persecution of the Jews in Europe, 1933-1945
New York: Bantam, 1973, 224 pp. Paper.

Pictorial history with a brief introduction. Especially recommended for students with reading difficulties. EJS

Studies

Apenszlak, Jacob, editor
The Black Book of Polish Jewry: An Account of the Martyrdom of Polish Jewry Under the Nazi Occupation
New York: Howard Fertig, 1982, xvi + 343 pp.

Originally published in 1943 as the first account of the destruction of the Jews of Poland, this book remains a classic documentary of the events under the German occupation of Poland. The second part of the book records the material and spiritual contributions of Polish Jewry which have been lost due to Nazi persecution. A valuable chronological account, based on eyewitness affidavits, official reports, and original documents. JSC

Bauer, Yehuda and Nathan Rotenstreich, editors
The Holocaust as Historical Experience
New York: Holmes & Meier, 1981, 288 pp. Paper.

A broad presentation of the state of historical research on the Holocaust, culled from materials presented at a conference on the Holocaust in New York in March 1975. The three sections, entitled, "Background," "Witnesses and Case Studies," and "The Judenrat and the Jewish Response," each contain essays utilizing a variety of approaches to the topic. The volume is written specifically for university students and teachers. Among the contributors: Saul Friedlaender, Jacob Katz, Raul Hilberg, Isaiah Trunk, and Uriel Tal. C

Friedman, Philip
Roads to Extinction:
Essays on the Holocaust
Edited by Ada June Friedman. Introduction by Salo Wittmayer Baron.
Philadelphia: Jewish Publication Society, 1980, xiv + 610 pp.

Twenty-four essays written between 1945 and 1960 by the "father of Holocaust history." Parts I and II deal with segregation and discrimination and some of the essays include: The Jewish Badge and the Yellow Star in the Nazi Era, The Lublin Reservation and the Madagascar Plan, Rulers of the Ghettos, Social Conflict in the Ghetto, Ukrainian-Jewish Relations, The Extermination of the Gypsies, Was There Another Germany? Aspects of Resistance and Righteous Gentiles. "The Destruction of the Jews of Lwow 1941-1944" remains the definitive work on what happened to this community. Part III deals with methodological problems and includes an overview on problems of research on the Holocaust which can well serve as a detailed course outline for teachers. SC

Grobman, Alex and Daniel Landes, editors; Sybil Milton, associate editor
Genocide: Critical Issues of the Holocaust
Los Angeles and Chappaqua, NY: Simon Wiesenthal Center and Rossel Books, 1983,
501 pp.

This companion volume to the film "Genocide" by the Wiesenthal Center consists of specially commissioned brief articles covering a wide range of Holocaust scholarship by experts in the field. Among the areas rarely covered: Jane Gerber on Sephardic and Oriental Jews, and one on Jewish religious leadership in Germany by David Ellenson. Recommended for teachers. SC

Braham, Randolph L.
The Politics of Genocide:
The Holocaust in Hungary
New York: Columbia University Press, 1981, 1269 pp. 2 Volumes.

Volume 1 includes the history of the Jewish community in Hungary after World War I and examines the various governments from the early 1930's on when the political climate shifted to Proto-Fascism. Braham examines the increasingly anti-Semitic policies and legislation, the formation of a labor service system – all before the Nazis occupied Hungary in 1944. He then goes on to describe the destructive process by the Third Reich of Hungary's 725,000 Jews: the imposed Jewish Council, pauperization and ghettoization. Volume 2 describes and analyzes the deportation process, including separate regional studies, attempts at rescue and resistance, the attitude and reactions of the Christian churches, international reaction and intervention; and finally liberation, restitution and retribution. Indices include source materials and the subject index is a very useful one. This is a major study and has been called the definitive account of the Holocaust in Hungary. Upper high school level students should have little trouble with this. Illustrated. SC

Ehrenberg, Ilya and Vasily Grossman
The Black Book: The Ruthless Murder of Jews by German-Fascist Invaders throughout the Temporarily-Occupied Regions of the Soviet Union and in the Death Camps of Poland during the War of 1941-1945
Translated from the Russian by John Glad and James S. Levine.
New York: Holocaust Library/Schocken, 1982,
595 pp. Also paper. (ADL)

A collection of World War II documents and eyewitness accounts of the destruction of

Soviet Jews. Prepared by the editors near the end of the war, the book was banned by Stalin in 1948, emerging in Israel in 1965, and finally published by Yad Vashem in 1980 (in Russian). An important and emotionally intense source, although it bears the mark of Soviet propaganda. JSC

Fein, Helen
Accounting for Genocide: National Responses and Jewish Victimization During the Holocaust
New York: The Free Press/ Macmillan, 1979,
468 pp.; University of Chicago Press, 1984,
xxii + 469 pp. Paper.(ADL)

Examines the structure of social forces and contingencies that either checked or facilitated the destruction of Jews in various countries. Deals with the reasons for the Holocaust's initiation and the broader history of Christian anti-Semitism which paved the way for Nazism. Analyzes personal accounts by Jews from Warsaw, the Netherlands and Hungary and reconstructs the collective behavior, psychology and social history of Europe's Jewish communities. Asks many questions. C

Friedlander, Henry and Sybil Milton, editors
The Holocaust: Ideology, Bureaucracy and Genocide
Millwood, NJ: Kraus International Publications, 1981, 353 pp.

Papers by leading scholars and academicians (Hilberg, Conway, et al.) originally presented at Holocaust conferences in San Jose. Reflects a trend to integrate the study of the Holocaust into the larger field of Nazi Germany and World War II. Among the topics covered: aspects of life in Weimer Germany; the professions in Nazi Germany; manipulation of language and art; anti-Nazi elites in Nazi-occupied Europe; U.S. government and popular response; after the Holocaust – in Christian theology, the university and the arts. C

Aizik Feder, *Seated Man with Beret, 1942*

Gutman, Yisrael and Livia Rothkirchen, editors
The Catastrophe of European Jewry: Antecedents—History—Reflections
Jerusalem: Yad Vashem, 1976, 757 pp.

Table of Contents: The Origins of Modern Anti-Semitism; The Jewish Question in Modern Anti-Semitic Literature; Anti-Christian Anti-Semitism; The Universal Significance of Modern Anti-Semitism; European Jewry Before and After Hitler; The Holocaust; The Origins and Development of Fascist Anti-Semitism in Italy (1922-1945); The Netherlands and Auschwitz; The "Final Solution" in its Last Stages; The Dignity of the Destroyed; The Day-to-Day Stand of the Jews; The Fate of the Children in the Warsaw Ghetto; The Attitude of the Judenrats to the Problems of Armed Resistance Against the Nazis; Adam Czerniakow; The Man and his Diary; Jewish Armed Resistance in Eastern Europe; The Jewish Fighting Organization–Z.O.B.; Betar's Role in the Warsaw Ghetto Uprising; The Warsaw Ghetto Uprising in the Light of a Hitherto Unpublished Official German Report; The "Righteous Among the Nations" and their Part in the Rescue of Jews; The Holocaust and the Struggle of the Yishuv as Factors in the Establishment of the State of Israel; Problems of Research on the European Jewish Catastrophe; The Holocaust in Jewish Historiography; The Mission of the Survivors; The Hiding God of History; Chronological Table of Events 1933-1945. SC

Katz, Robert
Black Sabbath: A Journey Through a Crime Against Humanity
New York: Macmillan, 1979, 398 pp.

A documented, compelling history of the Saturday in 1943 when over a thousand of Rome's Jews were rounded up for Auschwitz.
JS

Marrus, Michael and Robert O. Paxton
Vichy France and the Jews
New York: Basic Books, 1981, 432 pp.

An important account of the Vichy regime's treatment of the Jews. The authors establish that it was French anti-Semites and not Germans who initiated the Vichy anti-Semitic legislation. A well-argued and well-written scholarly work. C

Ringelblum, Emmanuel
Polish-Jewish Relations During the Second World War
Translated by Dafna Allon, et al.
New York: Howard Fertig, 1976, 330 pp.

A Warsaw Jew and a trained historian, Ringelblum was determined to systematically and accurately record what was happening to Polish Jewry during World War II. This volume, which includes information on almost all aspects of Polish-Jewish relations, is made even more valuable by the introduction and postscript by Joseph Kermish and the rich footnotes by Kermish and Shmuel Krakowski, both of whom edited the posthumous manuscript. Ringelblum states in his conclusion: "On the basis of this material we are bound to observe that the majority of the Polish people have been passive spectators of the mass murder of Jews by the Germans; that they have not been able to bring themselves to take a single step in defense of their fellow-citizens. Some elements of the Polish community have even actively taken measures against the Jews. . . Here and there, however, individuals can be found perhaps even small groups, who helped the Jews." SC

Robinson, Jacob, editor
The Holocaust and After: Sources and Literature in English
Jerusalem: Israel Universities Press, 1973, 353 pp.
Distributed by Transaction Books, New Brunswick, NJ.

The 12th volume in the monumental bibliographical series on the Holocaust sponsored by Yad Vashem Martyrs' and Heroes' Memorial Authority, Jerusalem, and YIVO Institute for Jewish Research, New York. Over 6,600 entries. Annotations are selective. Includes books, articles in other languages, scripts of films and television plays, informative reviews in English of books in other languages and review-essays on important books. General journals of opinion were not systematically screened, although some did find a place in this volume. Entries through 1970 with a supplement including some for 1971. The starting place for the serious student wishing to do research in this field. For every library. C

Sherwin, Byron L. and Susan G. Ament, editors
Encountering the Holocaust: An Interdisciplinary Survey
Chicago: Impact Press, 1979, 502 pp.

A useful (if somewhat uneven) survey of the literature in the field of history, sociology, political science, international law, psychology, literature, drama, film, music, art, theology, and philosophy. Much of the material is presented in the form of bibliographic essays. The section on moral implications includes various teaching models. Good reference for teachers and serious students. C

Tokayer, Marvin and Mary Sagmaster Swartz
Desperate Voyages
New York: Dell, 1980,
287 pp. Paper.

Between 1934 and 1940 a secret plan was devised by the Japanese government which might have saved large numbers of Jews. The Japanese wanted Jewish technicians, experts and industrialists to settle in Manchuria to develop the area into a buffer zone against the U.S.S.R. Why? Because they mistakenly accepted the forged Protocols of the Elders of Zion as accurately portraying Jews and they grossly overestimated the importance and influence of Jews in world economics and politics. A bizarre story told with the assistance of Jewish refugees who reached Japan before Pearl Harbor. Original title: *The Fugu Plan.* JSC

Trunk, Isaiah
Jewish Responses to Nazi Persecution
New York: Stein and Day, 1981,
384 pp. Paper. (ADL)

Examines the daily norms of life for Jews under Nazi tyranny, the structure of Jewish communities and the modes of personal and collective struggle engaged in by Nazism's victims. The author, Chief Archivist of the YIVO Institute for Jewish Research, gives a comprehensive survey of significant manifestations of Jewish life during the Holocaust

through 62 eyewitness accounts by survivors. The book also focuses on the behavior of the non-Jewish "host" peoples in whose countries the Nazis carried out their policies. SC

Yad Vashem Studies, Vol. I
Edited by Benzion Dinur and Shaul Esh.
Jerusalem, 1957, 183 pp.

Contents: Problems Confronting "Yad Vashem" in its Work of Research; Bibliographical Problems of the "Pinkas Hakehilloth"; On the Nazi Vocabulary; The Activities of Central Jewish Organizations Following Hitler's Rise to Power; On the Underground Press in the Warsaw Ghetto; The Rescue of Jews with the Aid of Passport and Citizenship Papers of Latin American States; Why No Separate Jewish Partisan Movement Was Established During World War II. SC

Yad Vashem Studies, Vol. II
Edited by Shaul Esh.
Jerusalem, 1958,
334 pp.

Contents: The Beginnings of Anti-Semitism in Independent Lithuania; The Crucial Year 1938; Between Discrimination and Extermination; Preliminary and Methodological Problems of the Research on the Jewish Catastrophe in the Nazi Period; Glimpses on the History of Jews in Occupied France; The

National Representation of Jews in Germany; The German Foreign Office and the Palestine Question in the Period 1933-1939; The Role of the Gestapo in Obstructing and Promoting Jewish Emigration; The Jewish Self-Administration in Ghetto Shargorod (Transnistria); The March of Death from Serbia to Hungary (September, 1944) and the Slaughter of Cservenka; The Underground Archives of the Bialystok Ghetto. SC

Yad Vashem Studies, Vol. III
Edited by Shaul Esh.
Jerusalem, 1959,
323 pp.

Contents: Modern Anti-Semitism and its Effect on the Jewish Question; The Promotion of Anti-Semitism through the Abuse of Democratic and Socialist Concepts; Problems of Research on the Jewish Catastrophe; Problems Related to the Study of the Jewish Resistance Movement in the Second World War; A Basis for Historical Research Concerning the Jewish Population Among the Nazi Occupation; The Role of Interviewing in the Research of the Holocaust Period; Problems Arising out of Research into the History of Jewish Refugees in the U.S.S.R. during the Second World War; The Anti-Nazi Boycott Movement in the United States; Jewish Education Under National Socialism; The French Central Jewish Consistory during the Second World War; The Central Jewish Organizations in Berlin during the Pogrom of November 1938; Problems of Disease in the Warsaw Ghetto; On the Catastrophe of the Thracian Jews; The Extermination of Two Ukrainian Jewish Communities. SC

Yad Vashem Studies, Vol. IV
Edited by Shaul Esh.
Jerusalem, 1960,
340 pp.

Contents: The Attitude of the Fascist Regime to the Jews in Italy; The Catholic Church and Italian Jewry under the Fascists; "Action"; Jewish Literature in the Soviet Union during the Holocaust Period to 1948; The Jews in the Soviet Partisan Movement; Exile in Mauritius; Documents on the Struggle of Rumanian Jewry for its Rights During the Second World War; Activities Organized by German Jewry during the Years 1933-1945. SC

Yad Vashem Studies, Vol. V
Edited by Nathan Eck and Aryeh Leon Kubovy.
Jerusalem, 1963,
432 pp.

Contents: Can Transgression Have an Agent? On the Moral-Judicial Problem of the Eichmann Trial; The Individual and Personal Responsibility; The Mentality of the SS Murderous Robots; Cross-Examining War Criminals; The

Hungarian Deportations in the Light of the Eichmann Trial; The Land of Israel in the Life of the Ghetto as Reflected in the Illegal Warsaw Ghetto Press; 25 Examples of Nazi-Idiom; The British Press and the Holocaust; Adjustment of Detainees to Camp and Ghetto Life and their Subsequent Readjustment to Normal Society; Magical Thinking Among the Jews During the Nazi Occupation; The Concept "Crime Against the Jewish People" in the Light of International Law; From S. Szajnkinder's Diary; The Jews in Berlin in the Year 1943; The Allies and the Resistance. SC

Yad Vashem Studies, Vol. VI
Edited by Nathan Eck and Aryeh Leon Kubovy.
Jerusalem, 1967,
436 pp.

Contents: The Silence of Pope Pius XII and the Beginning of the "Jewish Document"; Vatican Policy and the "Jewish Problem" in "Independent" Slovakia (1939-1945); Adam Czerniakow – the Man and his Supreme Sacrifice; From the Nazi Vocabulary; Designs for Anti-Jewish Policy in Germany up to the Nazi Rule; Leo Baeck and Contemporary History; The Destruction of the Jews of Odessa in the Light of Rumanian Documents; Political and Diplomatic Activities for the Rescue of the Jews of Northern Transylvania; The Rulers of Fascist Rumania; Scandinavian Countries to the Rescue of Concentration Camp Prisoners; Jewish Self-Defense and Resistance in France During World War II; How the Jews of Gruziya in Occupied France were Saved; Rescue of Jews of Bukharan, Iranian and Afghan Origin in Occupied France (1940-1944); Testimony of Herman F. Graebe; Extract from the Diary of Abraham Levin; Daily Record Sheet of the Jewish Police in the Czestochowa Ghetto (1941-1942). SC

Yad Vashem Studies, Vol. VII
Edited by Livia Rothkirchen.
Jerusalem, 1968,
238 pp.

Contents: Jewish Resistance and the European Resistance Movement; Eulogy on Shaul Esh; The Establishment of the "Reichsvereinigung der Juden in Deutschland" and its Main Activities; The Netherlands and Auschwitz; The Holocaust in Jewish Historiography; Spiritual Resistance in Holocaust Literature; The Bulgarian Exception – A Reassessment of the Salvation of the Jewish Community; Hehalutz in Theresienstadt; Hungary – An Asylum for the Refugees of Europe; The Organizational Structure of the Jewish Councils in Eastern Europe; Reflections on the Diary of Adam Czerniakow; Emmanuel Ringelblum's Notes hitherto Unpublished; Reflections on the Congress for the Prevention of

Genocide; The YIVO Colloquium on the Judenraete during the Nazi Period; The Convention on the Problems of Jewish Resistance during the Period of Holocaust; Testimonies and Recollections about Activities Organized by German Jewry during the Years 1933-1945. SC

Yad Vashem Studies, Vol. VIII
Edited by Livia Rothkirchen.
Jerusalem, 1970,
232 pp.

Contents: The "Final Solution" in its Last Stages; Spanish Nationals in Greece and their Fate during the Holocaust; Rescue Efforts with the Assistance of International Organizations; Budapest Jewry in the Summer of 1944; On the Threshold of Liberation – Reminiscences; The Initial Organization of the Holocaust Survivors in Bavaria; The Last Days of the Gross-Breesen Training Center; Silence in the American Textbooks; The Jewish Historical Institute in Warsaw. SC

Yad Vashem Studies, Vol. IX
Edited by Livia Rothkirchen.
Jerusalem, 1973,
353 pp.

Contents: The Warsaw Ghetto Uprising in the Light of a Hitherto Unpublished Official German Report; The Genesis of the Resistance in the Warsaw Ghetto;

American Diplomats in Berlin (1933-1939) and their Attitude to the Nazi Persecution of the Jews; Public Opinion in Western Europe and the Evian Conference of July 1938; Prelude to the Holocaust in Hungary; The Czechoslovak Government-in-Exile; Concentration of Refugees in Vilna on the Eve of the Holocaust; Rescue Operations through Vilna; "Policy of the Third Reich in Conquered Poland"; The Holocaust in the Encyclopedia Judaica; "Memorial Books" as a Source for Research into the History of Jewish Communities in Europe. SC

Yad Vashem Studies, Vol. X
Edited by Livia Rothkirchen.
Jerusalem, 1974,
326 pp.

Contents: In Memoriam Ben-Zion Dinur (1884-1973); The Controversial Stand of the Joodse Raad in the Netherlands: Lodewijk E. Visser's Struggle; The Role of the Jewish Council in Hungary; The Intelligence Aspect of the Joel Brand Mission; The Dispute over the Leadership of German Jewry (1932-1938); The Treatment of the Holocaust in West German Textbooks; On the Pathogenesis of the Anti-Semitism of Sebastian Brunner (1814-1893); Select British Documents on the Illegal Immigration to Palestine (1939-1940); Select Bibliography on Judenraete Under Nazi Rule. SC

Yad Vashem Studies, Vol. XI
Edited by Livia Rothkirchen.
Jerusalem, 1976,
384 pp.

Contents: The "Duce" and the
Jews; Italian Jewry under Fascism
1922-1945; An Overall Plan for
Anti-Jewish Legislation in the Third
Reich?; The Zionist Character of the
"Self-Government" of Terezin
(Theresienstadt); The Last Letters of
the Brandt-Meyer Family from
Berlin; The Impact of the Nazi
Racial Decrees on the University of
Heidelberg; American Non-
Sectarian Refugee Relief
Organizations (1933-1945); Soviet
Media on the Fate of Jews in Nazi-
Occupied Territory (1939-1941);
The "Final Solution" in Lithuania in
the Light of German Documenta-
tion; Estonian Jews in the U.S.S.R.
(1941-1945); The Plight of Jewish
Refugees from Czechoslovakia in
the U.S.S.R.; Kristallnacht at the
Dinslaken Orphanage. SC

Yad Vashem Studies, Vol. XII
Edited by Livia Rothkirchen.
Jerusalem, 1977,
387 pp.

Contents: Trends in Holocaust
Research; Jewish Policy and the
German Foreign Office (1939-
1940); The Reaction of the Jewish
Public in Germany to the Nurem-
berg Laws; The Diplomatic
Negotiations over the Transfer of
Jewish Children from Croatia to
Turkey and Palestine in 1943; The

Treatment of Hungarian Jews in
German-Occupied Europe; Some
Aspects of the History of the Jews
in Subcarpathian Ruthenia;
Relations between Poland and Ger-
many and their Impact on the
Jewish Problem in Poland (1935-
1938); Jews in General Ander's
Army in the Soviet Union; The Fate
of Jewish Prisoners of War in the
September 1939 Campaign; Jewish
Leadership in Occupied Poland.
SC

Yad Vashem Studies, Vol. XIII
Edited by Livia Rothkirchen.
Jerusalem, 1979,
424 pp.

Contents: On the Study of the
Holocaust and Genocide; On
Racism and Anti-Semitism in
Occultism and Nazism; Hitler and
the Genesis of the "Final Solution";
British Government Policy towards
Jewish Refugees (November 1937-
September 1939); Zionist Policy
and the Fate of European Jewry
(1939-1942); Anglo-Jewish
Leadership and the British Govern-
ment; European Jewry and the
Palestine Question; Alfred Rosen-
berg and the "Final Solution" in the
Occupied Soviet Territories; Czech
Attitudes Towards the Jews during
the Nazi Regime; Attempts to
Obtain Shanghai Permits in 1941;
A Case of Rescue Priority during
the Holocaust; The Reminiscences
of Victor Kugler – the "Mr. Kraler"
of Anne Frank's Diary; Pre-War

Reactions to Nazi Anti-Jewish
Policies in the Jewish Press.
SC

Anthologies and Readers

*Chartock, Roselle and Jack Spencer,
editors*
**The Holocaust Years: Society on
Trial**
New York: Bantam, 1978,
224 pp. Paper. ADL

Developed and tested by high
school teachers. Divided into six
parts – What happened?; Victims
and victimizers; How and why?;
What does the Holocaust reveal
about the individual and society?;
Aftermath; Could it happen again?
Eighty-eight brief selections, includ-
ing eyewitness accounts and
memoirs, by William L. Shirer, Lucy
Dawidowicz, Elie Wiesel, Anne
Frank, Rudolf Hoess, Albert Speer,
Yevgeny Yevtushenko, Gordon
Allport, Robert Ardrey, B.F. Skinner,
and many others. Based on unit
taught in Monument Mountain
Regional High School, Great
Barrington, MA. Good introduction.
JS

Dawidowicz, Lucy S., editor
A Holocaust Reader
New York: Behrman House, 1976,
397 pp. Paper.

Parallels the author's narrative, *The*

War Against The Jews (see above).
Sixty-seven selections: Nazi decrees
and reports, Jewish communal
records, diaries, letters, etc.
Introductory essay: "On Studying
Holocaust Documents." JSC

Eisenberg, Azriel
**The Lost Generation: Children in
the Holocaust**
New York: The Pilgrim Press, 1982,
380 pp.

120 selections by and about
children from Germany in the
1920's through the post-war years.
Includes all aspects of the
Holocaust and its aftermath. A
companion to *Witness to the
Holocaust.* EJS

Eisenberg, Azriel
Witness to the Holocaust
New York: Pilgrim Press, 1981,
649 pp.

Over 600 readings, most of them
eyewitness accounts, covering all
aspects of the Holocaust. Divided
into twenty-five topics, includes
introduction and bibliography for
each section. JSC

Eliach, Yaffa
Hasidic Tales of the Holocaust
New York: Oxford University Press, 1982, 266 pp. Also paper. (ADL hardcover)

Based on interviews and oral histories, this collection of 89 stories is the first anthology of Hasidic stories about the Holocaust, and the first ever in which women play a large role—not merely as daughters, sisters or wives but because of their own faith, conviction, and moral courage.
JSC

Friedlander, Albert H., editor
**Out of The Whirlwind:
A Reader of Holocaust Literature**
New York: Union of American Hebrew Congregations, 1968; Schocken, 1976, 544 pp. Paper.

Lengthy excerpts from novels, memoirs, diaries. Section on philosophical-theological issues. Recommended for literature classes. Some selections (especially by Hans Jonas) for serious teachers. SC

Friedmann, Ina R.
Escape or Die: True Stories of Young People Who Survived the Holocaust
Reading, MA: Addison-Wesley, 1982, 160 pp. (ADL)

Twelve survivors each from a different country, recount their experiences. Told simply and straightforwardly. Illustrated.
EJS

Glatstein, Jacob, et al., editors
Anthology of Holocaust Literature
New York: Temple Books/Atheneum, 1972, 412 pp. Paper.

Sixty-five selections, all by victims and eyewitnesses. A moving collection. JSC

Gutman, Yisrael, Yitzhak Arad and Abraham Margaliot, editors
Documents on the Holocaust
Jerusalem: Yad Vashem, 1981, 504 pp. (ADL)

More than 200 documents including Nazi decrees and legislation, secret protocols, Jewish responses to discrimination, expropriation and deportation. Comprehensive introduction. SC

Haas, Gerda
**These I Do Remember:
Fragments from the Holocaust**
Freeport, Maine: The Cumberland Press, 1982, 238 pp.

Using the memoirs of others and her own story, the author introduces the reader to the fears, the suffering and the humanity of the victims, and the brutality of the Nazis. The listing of world events—major and minor—provides a dramatic juxtaposition to the words of the memoirists and diarists, and her narrative places them in historical perspective. A loving memorial and an urgent reminder. JS

Hilberg, Raul, editor
Documents of Destruction: Germany and Jewry: 1933-1945
New York: New Viewpoints, 1971, xii + 243 pp.

Official German documents and Jewish autobiographical material. One example:

L Ho/S   Poznan July 16, 1941

Memorandum
Subject: Solution of the Jewish question

1. All the Jews of Warthe province will be taken to a Camp for 300,000 Jews which will be erected in barracks form as close as possible to the coal precincts and which will contain barracks-like installations for economic enterprises, tailor shops, shoe manufacturing plants, etc. . . .
2. This winter there is a danger that not all of the Jews can be fed anymore. One should weigh honestly, if the most humane solution might not be to finish off those of the Jews who are not employable by means of some quick-working device. At any rate, that would be more pleasant than to let them starve to death.
3. For the rest, the proposal was made that in this camp all the Jewish women, from whom one could still expect children, should be sterilized so that the Jewish problem may actually be solved completely with this generation.

Edited with commentary. JSC

Hirt-Manheimer, Aron, editor
Keeping Posted
Five teacher editions related to the Holocaust
New York: Union of American Hebrew Congregations.

Five issues of this magazine intended for grades 8 – 12.

1. Aspects of the Holocaust and Hitler's War Against the Jews (Feb. 1976). 2. Art of the Holocaust (Jan. 1978). 3. The Christian Conscience (Oct. 1978). 4. Children of the Holocaust (Nov. 1979). 5. The Shtetl (April, 1975). Each issue is 24 pages and is richly illustrated. Each includes an eight-page teacher's guide prepared by Alan D. Bennet.

Korman, Gerd, editor
Hunter and Hunted: Human History of the Holocaust
New York: Delta, 1973, 320 pp. Paper.

From the "refugee problem" of the late 1930's through the war and liberation. Reports, excerpts, poetry, fiction. SC

Szajkowski, Zosa
**An Illustrated Source Book
on the Holocaust**
3 volumes. Oversize.
New York: KTAV. Vol. I, 1977, 155
pp.; Vol. II, 1979, 178 pp.; Vol. III,
1979, 183 pp.

Hundreds of photographs, re-
productions of Nazi and anti-
Semitic propaganda cartoons,
statements, artifacts, documents
from Germany, France, U.S.S.R.
Class resource. EJS

Rabbinic Responsa

Kirschner, Robert (ed.)
**Rabbinic Responsa in the
Holocaust Era**
Translated with introduction and
notes by Robert Kirschner
New York: Schocken, 1985,
206 pp. Cloth.

Good introduction to the interior
world of observant Jews. Kirschner
has selected 14 Holocaust-related
responsa (questions and answers
on Jewish law asked of rabbis) from
the many hundred that are found in
scholarly collections. These concern
events of both ritual and moral
significance. Kirschner has provided
the reader with a source book. He
includes the historical and halakhic
(Jewish law) contexts, and provides
references for further inquiry. Some
of the questions: Must a Jew, hiding from the Germans in a ghetto
bunker, repent for inadvertently
smothering a crying infant to avoid
detection? Is assignment in the
direction of the crematoria suffi-
cient proof of death? Are ghetto
expediency marriages valid? Is it
permissible to sterilize an insane
woman (in compliance with Nazi
legislation)? Especially recommended for those interested in theology, cultural history. C

Oshry, Ephraim
Responsa from the Holocaust
New York: Judaica Press, 1983,
260 pp. Cloth.

Rabbi Oshry was one of the few
rabbinical authorities to survive the
Kovno ghettò. This volume is an
abridged English version of his five-
volume work, *Questions and
Answers from Out of the Depth.*

"During those dark years I noted down, in pencil, on scraps of paper torn from concrete sacks, the questions asked of me by my fellow Jews, and the answers I gave them, concerning problems of Jewish religious observance amidst the hardships and dangers of ghetto life. I placed these notes into tin cans, which I buried in the soil of the ghetto in the hope that they would be found after the war and serve as a historic record of how, no matter what befell, the Jews of the Kovno ghetto were determined to live by the laws of the Torah. After the liberation of Kovno in August, 1944, I unearthed these cans and found their contents happily intact."

The 112 responsa deal with a wide range of ritual, moral, and ethical issues. Although written in a deceptively simple style, the collection demands that the reader have a fairly thorough knowledge of Jewish traditions and law.

A good source book for Jewish high school and adult education classes in halakah and/or the Holocaust. SC

David Brainin, *Concert Program, 1942*

Memoirs

Hoffman, Judy
Joseph and Me: In the Days of the Holocaust
Hoboken, NJ: KTAV, 1979, 80 pp. Paper.

The author describes her experiences as a German-Jewish child living in hiding with a Dutch-Christian family in Amsterdam. Additional text and photos include further details of the Holocaust. Some of the photo captions have minor inaccuracies. EJ

AUDIO-VISUAL

The Eighty-First Blow

120 minutes (shorter version, 90 minutes)/black-and-white/Hebrew and English subtitles/Alden Films and some local Israeli consulates.

Documentary using footage and stills shot by the Nazis. The narrative is from testimony at the Eichmann trial. Rough going. SC

Genocide

52 minutes/color/ADL.

Perhaps the definitive film on the Holocaust. Part of the British-produced "World at War" TV series, "Genocide" is the history of the Final Solution from the 1920's, when waves of anti-Semitism spread through Germany, to 1945, when the remnants of European Jewry were liberated from concentration camps. Extraordinary film footage, much of it never seen before, and interviews with concentration camp survivors as well as Germans who were directly involved in implementing the Final Solution convey the methodical insanity of theNazi era and the near total destruction of the Jewish people. Seeing and hearing the living who tell of the dying remains a haunting experience for anyone who has viewed the film. Israel, though never mentioned, emerges as a land of refuge for the Jewish people, since

many of the interviews with survivors were filmed there. Narrated by Sir Laurence Olivier. SC

Holocaust

13 parts/35-minutes each/color/Learning Corp. of America

The docu-drama series produced by NBC-TV. JSC

The Holocaust

24 minutes/black-and-white/Alden

Documentary overview, using Nazi film footage and stills, which places the events of the Holocaust in historical perspective. Produced by Yad Vashem. JSC

The Holocaust

2-part filmstrip/color/LP or cassette/teacher's guide/Social Studies School Services and Audio-Visual Narrative Arts

Examines the Holocaust from two aspects: the actual experience of the victims, on the one hand, and the historical background of European anti-Semitism, Hitler's personal beliefs, and the elaborate organization set up in Nazi Germany for extermination of an entire people, on the other hand. Most of the visuals are photographs from the period of Nazi Germany and World War II. JS

The Holocaust: 1933-1945
20 posters (23" x 29")/black-and-white/ADL

A series of photographic black-and-white posters designed by Allon Schoener, creator of exhibits for the Metropolitan Museum of Art and The Smithsonian Institution. The series begins with pre-Holocaust Jewish life in Europe, and goes on to depict the growth of Nazism and anti-Semitism, the ghettos, the death camps, liberation, the Nuremberg Trials, and ultimately the building of new lives in Israel. Includes Viewer's Guide and Suggestions for Display. JSC

The Holocaust and the Resistance:
An Artist's Personal Account of the Holocaust
Filmstrip or slide/cassette/color/Shimbal Studios

Paintings by Shimon Balitski, a survivor of the camps, depicting Jewish life from pre-World War II shtetl to liberation in 1945. JSC

Human Rights and the Holocaust
4 booklets/2 cassettes/6 transparencies/teacher's guide/Educational Activities and Social Studies School Service

Eight personal reminiscences told by Holocaust survivors. Four are on cassettes (2 per cassette) and four are in a book. The cassettes include: Hitler's Entrance into Vienna; Crystal Night; The Process of Dehumanization in the Concentration Camps – Dachau and Auschwitz; What America Means to Me. The short, simply written stories include: The Miracle – a young Aryan officer fights with his conscience and decides to save Jewish lives; The Escape – a family of Austrian Jews flees from the Nazis; Lilka – a story of love; and Voyage to Freedom – an escape from Nazi Europe and the difficult voyage to Palestine. Produced by Lillian Dubsky, a survivor. JS

Memorandum
58 minutes/black-and-white

To commemorate the 20th anniversary of their liberation from Nazi concentration camps, a group of survivors return to Germany. Their pilgrimage is recorded in this Canadian National Film board documentary which compares the Germany of the past with the present. The horrors of Auschwitz, Bergen-Belsen and Treblinka are contrasted with a contemporary court trial where the perpetrators of the Holocaust are set free and absolved from guilt in carrying out Goering's orders on the Final Solution. JSC

Nazi Holocaust: Series I
25 photographs/teacher's guide/Social Studies School Service

The pictures include German

soldiers and civilians, the Warsaw Ghetto, SS troops, liberated slave laborers, mass burials, Dachau, Auschwitz and Buchenwald concentration camps. Printed on 11" x 14" heavy glossy stock. SC

Nazi Holocaust: Series II
40 photographs/teacher's guide/ Social Studies School Service

The pictures include concentration camps, anti-Semitic activities in Germany, ghettos, German soldiers mistreating Jews, atrocities, guards, prisoners, officials, German citizens forced to view the dead, gas ovens, and the allies. Printed on 11" x 14" glossy stock. SC

Posters of the Holocaust Period
Perfection Form Company

Posters and sets of posters which illustrate the history of World War II and the concepts related to that period.

Self-Standing Exhibit on the Holocaust
American Federation of Jewish Fighters, Camp Inmates, Nazi Victims.

Thirty-three panels of photos and charts available on loan. Shipping charges.

Camps, Ghettos, In Hiding

Frozen to the lower edge of the cattle-car door, like very small icicles, the thin fingers of a child.

Lothar Kusche
People in Freight Cars

PUBLICATIONS

Reports and Studies

Abzug, Robert H.
Inside the Vicious Heart: Americans and the Liberation of Nazi Concentration Camps
New York: Oxford University Press, 1985, 175 pp. Cloth.

What was it like to be among the first to discover the nightmare of the Nazi concentration camps? How did those who liberated the camps react to the unexpected horror? Through reflection and the use of individual testimony, Abzug dramatically reconstructs the wide range of the liberators' complex responses, from initial numbness, to a questioning of a lifetime of beliefs, to the desire to forget and yet remember. SC

Arad, Yitzhak
Ghetto in Flames: The Struggle and Destruction of the Jews in Vilna in the Holocaust
Hoboken, NJ: KTAV, 1980; Holocaust Library, 1982, 500 pp. Paper. (ADL, paper)

A detailed and fully documented account of this community, once famous as the "Jerusalem of Lithuania." Among the topics dealt with: German military and civil administrations, internal organization of the ghetto, various "aktions" and liquidation programs, extermination tolls, resistance, life in the ghetto. Illustrated. SC

Berkovits, Eliezer
With God in Hell: Judaism in the Ghettos and Death Camps
New York: Sanhedrin Press, 1979, 166 pp.

A believing Jew and a philosopher, Berkovits tells how many in the ghettos and camps fought to retain their dignity through continued practice of Judaism, often transcending the reality in which they were engulfed. SC

Birnbaum, Israel
My Brother's Keeper: The Holocaust Through the Eyes of an Artist
New York: G. Putnam's Sons, 1985, 64 pp. Cloth.

The story of the Holocaust, and in particular, the story of the Warsaw Ghetto and its destruction, is told in a simply and engagingly written narrative and in a series of five striking and dramatic paintings: "The Warsaw Ghetto Streets, in 1943," "On Both Sides of the Ghetto Wall," "The Jewish Mother in the Ghetto," "The Jewish Children in the Ghettos and Death Camps," and "The Warsaw Ghetto Uprising — Heroism and Resistance." Literal, colorful, and fusing together human beings caught in various phases of murder and annihilation, these paintings are accessible to children who are 6-to-12-year-olds. The text draws the attention of readers to the content and symbolism of the story expressed in various parts of each canvas. EJ

Bor, Joseph
The Terezin Requiem
New York: Avon Bard, 1978, 119 pp. Paper.

Terezin, a "model" concentration camp, housed many artists. An account of the preparation, performance and outcome of Verdi's Requiem before an SS audience which included Eichmann. JSC

Charlotte Buresova, *The Cellist, c. 1943*

Donat, Alexander, editor
The Death Camp Treblinka:
A Documentary
New York: Holocaust Library, 1979,
320 pp. Also paper.
(ADL, also paper)

At least 700,000 and possibly
more than a million persons, pre-
dominantly Jews, but also a number of Gypsies, were killed at the
Treblinka extermination camp in
Poland. This book documents the
lives of the victims and the August
2, 1943 revolt. Only a thousand
were still alive when the uprising
put an end to the death factory.
Only two hundred managed to
break through to escape, and of
these, only sixty survived the war to
tell the story. SC

Friedman, Philip, editor
Martyrs and Fighters:
The Epic of the Warsaw Ghetto
New York: Praeger, 1954,
325 pp.

First-hand accounts on all aspects
of daily life in the ghetto from the
beginning of World War II to the
last day of the uprisings. Excellent
compilation. JSC

Kurtzman, Dan
The Bravest Battle:
The 28 Days of the Warsaw
Ghetto Uprising
New York: Putnam, 1976, 386 pp.;
Pinnacle Paper, 1978. (ADL paper)

Powerful, step-by-step account of
this historic battle. JSC

Schnabel, Ernst
Anne Frank: A Portrait in
Courage
New York: Harcourt Brace, 1958,
181 pp. Also paper.

The author reconstructs the life of
Anne Frank based on testimony of
42 witnesses and documents. An
important complement to the Diary.
JS

Schneider, Gertrude
Journey into Terror:
Story of the Riga Ghetto
New York: Irvington, 1981, 229 pp.

A dispassionate account by a
scholar-survivor (then a child).
Based on Nazi documents,
depositions, interviews with survivors – and the diary she kept during the days of the Riga Ghetto. On
October 25, 1941, all Jews living in
Riga, Latvia, were brought into the
ghetto. By November 9, approximately 28,000 including all the
women and children, had been
murdered by the Einsatzgruppen.
The ghetto was then repopulated
with transports of Jews from Germany, Austria and Czechoslovakia.
The Nazis separated the communities, so that Latvian Jews —all
male — were on one side, and
German-speaking Jewish families
were on the other. Includes information on education. Zionist and
cultural activities, romance. The
Riga Ghetto also fed and was part
of the satellite of concentration
work-death camps in the area. SC

Selzer, Michael
Deliverance Day:
The Last Hours at Dachau
Philadelphia and New York: Lippin-
cott, 1978, 252 pp.

An hour-by-hour account of the
liberation of 30,000 inmates at
Dachau in April 1945 by U.S. Army
troops. The author interviewed former inmates and American soldiers.
Includes photos of Dachau taken by
the soldiers. JSC

Stroop, Juergen
The Stroop Report:
The Jewish Quarter of Warsaw Is
No More!
Translated from the German by
Sybil Milton. Introduction by
Andrzej Wirth, Pantheon, 1980, n.p.

This official Nazi account of the
battle was originally bound in black
leather as a memento for S.S. Chief
Himmler. S.S. Major General Stroop
commanded the operation which
liquidated the ghetto. The report
consists of Stroop's introduction,
32 teletypes describing the daily
operations in macabre detail, and
photographs taken by the Nazis.
After the war, Stroop was hanged
by the government of Poland. (For a
fascinating account of Stroop after
the war, cf. "Conversations With a
Hangman", *Midstream*, Nov. 1980,
pp. 31-41) SC

Trunk, Isaiah
Judenrat
New York: Stein and Day, 1977,
Paper.

An examination of the role and
limitations of 450 Jewish councils,
their leaders, their choices and lack
of them. Includes their organization
structure (decentralization and cen-
tralization, dictatorial and collective
leadership); the degree of their representative qualities (continuation
with or severance from the prewar
representative bodies of the Jewish
communities); their political and
social composition; their activities
in the fields of ghetto economy,
welfare, hygiene, medical help and
religious affairs; their educational
and cultural work; their administrative and judicial functions; the
council employees; the Jewish
police; relations with other Jewish
organizations and with the resistance movement. Includes dis-
cussions of the painful postwar
afteraffects, and of the trials of surviving council members and ghetto
policemen. National Book Award.
Important source. SC

Louis Ascher, *A Group of Children Seated
in Front of the Barracks, c. 1944*

Ziemian, Joseph
The Cigarette Sellers of Three Crosses Square
New edition.
Translated from the Polish by
Janina David. Minneapolis: Lerner,
1975, 180 pp.; Avon, 1977, 140
pp. Paper. (ADL paper)

True story of a group of Jewish
children who managed to escape
from the Warsaw Ghetto in 1942
and survived in the Aryan section of
the Nazi-occupied city. Exciting,
moving. JS

Memoirs and Diaries

Adler, Stanislaw
Diary of Stanislaw Adler
Jerusalem and New York: Yad
Vashem and ADL, 1981.

From 1940 to 1943, the author, a
lawyer, was part of the Jewish
Council in Warsaw, first in the legal
department of the Jewish Police,
later as director of the Housing
Office. Realizing what the deportations meant, he escaped and was
hidden in the "Aryan" part of Warsaw. It was there in 1943 that he
wrote this remarkable document.
Adler writes about the working of
the Police, the Judenrat officials
(Czerniakow, et al.) and life and
death in the Ghetto. He survived
the war but in 1946, after the
pogrom in Kielce, Poland when
dozens of Jews who had returned
"home" were murdered by their
fellow Poles, Adler committed
suicide. An important and fascinating document. JSC

Baldwin, Margaret
The Boys Who Saved the Children
New York: Messner, 1981,
62 pp.

Ben Edelbaum describes the
courage and strength that held his
family together during the horror of
the Warsaw Ghetto and how a gift
the children made for the commandant's wife saved numbers of
ghetto children. . . for a while. Illustrated with photos from YIVO.
EJ

Cohen, Elie A.
The Abyss: A Confession
New York: W.W. Norton, 1973,
111 pp.

Brief, moving, simply written testimony by a Jewish prisoner-doctor confessing his shortcomings, but telling us that we, who were not there, have no right to judge.
SC

Delbo, Charlotte
**None of Us Will Return:
Auschwitz and After**
Boston: Beacon Press, 1968,
126 pp. Paper (ADL)

The author was a member of the French Resistance and sent to several concentration camps, ending up in Auschwitz. Her book has been called, "a tribute to the power of the imagination to evoke the inexpressible." She says, "I am no longer sure that what I have written is true, but I am sure that it happened." Powerful, provocative, poetic. SC

Donat, Alexander
**The Holocaust Kingdom: A
Memoir**
New York: Holocaust Library, 1978,
368 pp. Also paper. (ADL paper)

A journalist writes of life in the Warsaw Ghetto, the camps and his family's reentry into life after the war. Includes a chapter by his wife and one by the woman who hid his child. Well written; packed with information. SC

Fenelon, Fania
Playing for Time
New York: Berkley, 1983
262 pp. Paper.

The author was a cabaret singer and French resistance worker who was taken to Auschwitz and became a member of the women's orchestra in the camp. There, she played marches by day for the prisoners, and waltzes and "Madame Butterfly" at night for the Nazi guards. Made into a television feature film. See also *Music of Auschwitz* in A-V section below. SC

Ferderber-Salz, Bertha
And the Sun Kept Shining. . .
New York: Holocaust Library, 1980,
240 pp. Also paper. (ADL, also paper)

Until September 1, 1939, Bertha Ferderber lived quietly in Cracow, untouched by the course of world events. From there on we follow her in flight, in hiding, in narrow escapes, tortures, and in a struggle to rescue her children. Called a writer of superior talent. SC

Frank, Anne
**Anne Frank's Tales from the
Secret Annex**
Translated by Ralph Manheim and Michael Mok
New York: Washington Square Press, 1983, 156 pp. Paper.

More of Anne's sweetness, spirit and artistry is revealed in this collection of her essays, stories, and memoirs — many found only after her father's death, and newly published. JS

Gurdus, Luba Krugman
The Death Train
New York: Holocaust Library, 1979, 165 pp. Also paper. (ADL)

The author, a survivor of Maidanek and an artist, watches her family's life plagued by terror and disrupted by separations, deportations and death. Across from their windows are the tracks on which the Death Train rolls its human cargo to the camp at Belzec. The Train becomes the obsession of the author's four-year-old son, whose fear is sealed in a drawing included in the book. Includes many sketches by the author. JSC

Hart, Kitty
Return to Auschwitz
New York: Atheneum, 1983, 178 pp. Also paper.

Memoir of a young Polish Jewish girl's struggle for survival, from her hometown of Bielsko to Lublin's ghetto, prison in Germany, and almost two years in Auschwitz. Years later, she returns to Auschwitz with her grown son, and records the melding of her past and present. JSC

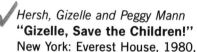

Hersh, Gizelle and Peggy Mann
"Gizelle, Save the Children!"
New York: Everest House, 1980, 319 pp.

The Hersh family, with four daughters and one son, lived in Bixad, a resort town in Hungary, with a population of 7,000 including some 600 Jews. They were deported to Auschwitz in the Summer of 1944. Gizelle, 17, was the oldest child. Her mother had a premonition of what would happen and made her promise to save the children. A story of the roundup, the ghetto, the box-car to Auschwitz-Birkenau, the slave labor camps, and finally, for a few — survival. JS

Leon Landau, *Portrait of a Young Man, 1943*

✓ *Heyman, Eva*
The Diary of Eva Heyman
Translated from the Hebrew by
Moshe M. Kohn.
Introduction and notes by Dr. Judah
Marton.
Jerusalem: Yad Vashem, 1974,
124 pp. (ADL)

From her 13th birthday on February
13, 1944, to May 30, 1944, 3 days
before she was deported from her
native town in Hungary to
Auschwitz, Eva kept her diary. She
grew up in an assimilated cos-
mopolitan family and describes
events that took place in the town
and in her personal life. A touching
book by a young girl, whose last
entry indicates that she knew what
her fate would be, and who wanted
desperately to live. JSC

*Hilberg, Raul, Stanislaw Staron and
Josef Kermisz, editors*
**The Warsaw Diary of Adam
Czerniakow: Prelude to Doom**
New York: Stein and Day, 1982,
448 pp. Paper. (ADL)

For nearly three years Adam Czerniakow was chairman of the Warsaw
Judenrat — the Nazi-appointed
Jewish community council and
"mayor" of the Warsaw Ghetto.
From Sept. 6, 1939 to July 23,
1942, when he committed suicide,
he kept a secret journal of that city-
within-a-city before its half-million
people were deported to the death
camp at Treblinka. Czerniakow's
personal dealings with the German

authorities and his central role in
the council provide this diary with
an accuracy of detail and intimacy
of acquaintance possible to no
other participant in this chapter of
the Holocaust. The editors'
introduction provides a valuable
framework for this important testimony. Illustrated. SC

✓ *Jackson, Livia E. Bitton*
**Elli: Coming of Age in the
Holocaust**
New York: Times Books, 1983,
248 pp. Paper.

Experience of a 13-year-old girl
poet from Hungary. "Told with
breathtaking lucidity. . . her images
remain in the mind, beyond words.
Destined to join the classics of
Holocaust literature." — *Chicago
Tribune*. JSC

Kaplan, Chaim A.
**The Scroll of Agony:
The Warsaw Diary of Chaim A.
Kaplan**
Translated from the Hebrew and
edited by Abraham I. Katsch.
New York: Macmillan, 1981,
416 pp. Paper.

The last words in the Hebrew
manuscript, written on August 4,
1942: "If my life ends — what will
become of my diary?" Four months
after writing these words, Chaim
Kaplan died in Treblinka. But the
diary was preserved, found under
the rubble, and it gives a unique
view of the final days and nights of

the Warsaw Ghetto. Kaplan describes life from day to day — the
decisions of the Jewish Council, the
heroes and the villains, pathetic victims such as the "Hebrew-
Christians;" and all the while he is
dying of starvation. An invaluable
human document. JSC

Klein, Gerda Weissman
All But My Life
New York: Hill and Wang, 1971,
247 pp. Paper.

The author was fifteen when the
Nazis brought the war to the Polish
town in which she and her family
lived. This is the moving story of
her survival as a slave laborer, and
of others who did not survive.
JSC

Korczak, Janusz
a. Ghetto Diary
New York: Holocaust Library, 1978,
192 pp. Also paper.
Introduction (a lengthy prose poem)
by Aaron Zeitlin. (ADL, also paper)

b. The Warsaw Ghetto:
Memoirs of Janusz Korczak
Translated from the Polish with an
introduction by E.P. Kulawiec.
Washington, DC: University Press of
America, 1978,
128 pp. Paper.

c. The Ghetto Years
Translated from the Polish by Jerzy
Bachrach and Barbara Krywicka.
90-page introduction "The Final
Chapter" by Yitzhak Perils.

Translated from the Hebrew by
Avner Tomaschoff.
Israel: Ghetto Fighters' House,
1980, 264 pp. Paper.

Physician, novelist and, above all,
educator, Korczak, a Polish Jew,
was a living legend. He refused to
desert the children of the
orphanage he headed in the Warsaw Ghetto and went with them to
his and their death at Treblinka. The
diary is from his last years.
UNESCO proclaimed 1978 as the
International Janusz Korczak Year.
SC

Leitner, Isabella
Fragments of Isabella:
A Memoir of Auschwitz
Edited and with an epilogue by
Irving Leitner
New York: Crowell, 1978, 112 pp.;
Dell, 1983. Paper.

In May 1944, Isabella, her four sisters, her brother, and her mother
were rounded up along with other
Jews in a town in Hungary for
deportation to Auschwitz. They
struggled to survive, to build a
future free of bloodshed. A poetic
recapturing. JSC

Levi, Primo
Survival in Auschwitz:
The Nazi Assault on Humanity
Translated from the Italian by
Stuart Woolf
New York: Collier/Macmillan, 1961,
157 pp. (ADL paper)
(Original title in hardcover edition:
If This is a Man.)

An Italian-Jewish chemist, captured
by the Fascist militia in 1943,
interned because of partisan
activities, turned over to the Nazis
and shipped to Auschwitz. Excellent,
dispassionate witness account.
SC

Mermelstein, Mel
By Bread Alone:
The Story of A-4685
Second edition.
Published by Mel Mermelstein,
1981, 290 pp.

The only member of his immediate
family who survived the death
camps, the author recalls his
childhood in a village in the
Carpatho-Ukraine, the ghetto, concentration camps. Auschwitz-
Birkenau, Gross Rosen and
Buchenwald and his wanderings
after the liberation. Illustrated. SC

Muller, Phillip
Eyewitness Auschwitz:
Three Years in
the Gas Chambers
New York: Stein & Day, 1979,
180 pp.

A dispassionate, powerful account
of life, death and resistance in
Auschwitz written by a Slovakian Jew
who was a Sonderkommando — a
camp inmate assigned to work in
the crematoria. SC

Nomberg-Przytyk, Sara
Auschwitz: True Tales
From a Grotesque Land
Chapel Hill: University of North
Carolina Press, 1985,
185 pp. Cloth.

The simplicity and straightforward-
ness of these tales — composites
of history and imagination —
powerfully convey the moral and life
and death dilemmas of women
caught up in the whirlwind of
Auschwitz. The first chapter,
"Alienation," delicately records the
disdain (anti-Semitism?) of non-
Jewish women inmates and sets a
tone of isolation. The reader is
forced to reflect on whether or not
ordinary considerations are applicable. Teachers will find the Editor's
Afterword most helpful in placing
the "tales" in a larger context. SC

Novitch, Miriam, editor
Sobibor: Martyrdom and Revolt
New York: Holocaust Library, 1980,
168 pp. Paper (ADL)

On October 14, 1943, in Sobibor,
one of the smallest Nazi extermination camps, Jews revolted. They
overpowered the guards, seized the
armory, and, after an exchange of
shots with the camp garrison, fled.
Approximately 300 Jews escaped.
Thirty of the survivors tell of life in

the camp and of the revolt. Miriam Novitch is a member of the Ghetto Fighters' Kibbutz in Israel and is the curator of its Holocaust Museum. SC

Nyiszli, Miklos
Auschwitz: A Doctor's Eyewitness Account
New York: Crest/Fawcett, 1979, xvii + 222 pp. Paper.

An eyewitness account by a Jewish doctor who "volunteered to become a tool of the SS to stay alive." An account of the SS medical doctors, including the infamous Dr. Mengele, and their experiments. Conceptually easy. Interesting foreword by Bruno Bettelheim may present some difficulty. JSC

Oberski, Jona
Childhood: A Remembrance
Translated by Ralph Manheim
New York: Doubleday, 1983, 119 pp. Plume, 1984. Paper.

Thrust into a world where a child's test of belonging is to enter the house of the dead, young Jona struggles to make sense out of his new life in a concentration camp. Oberski does a remarkable job of separating the child's memories from his own adult understanding of the events he survived. Profoundly moving and searing. JSC

Ringelblum, Emmanuel
Notes From the Warsaw Ghetto: The Journal of Emmanuel Ringelblum
Edited and translated by Jacob Sloan.
New York: Schocken, 1974, 389 pp. Paper.

Day-by-day eyewitness accounts by a social historian who was the archivist of the Warsaw Ghetto. Ringelblum buried his notes in the ghetto before his execution by the Nazis in 1944. They were found in 1946 and 1950. JSC

Irene Awret, *Portrait of the Painter Azriel Awret, 1944*

Sandberg, Moshe
My Longest Year: In the Hungarian Labour Service and in the Nazi Camps
Translated from the Hebrew by S.C. Hyman.
Edited, with an historical survey by Livia Rothkirchen, Jerusalem: Yad Vashem, 1968, xxxiv + 114 pp. (ADL)

Written 10 years after his release from a German concentration camp, the account covers the author's life in his hometown from the time the German Army marched into Hungary in March, 1944, his mobilization in a Hungarian labor battalion and his incarceration in Muhldorf-Waldlager. SC

Stiffel, Frank
The Tale of the Ring: A Kaddish
Wainscott, N.Y.: Pushcart Press, 1984, 345 pp. Cloth.

In this powerful memoir, the author recounts a journey involving hiding, capture, escape, recapture, and eventual internment in Auschwitz. Thoughtful and gentle in his approach, Stiffel recalls his experiences with an amazing eye for detail. SC

Tillion, Germaine
Ravensbruck: An Eyewitness Account of a Women's Concentration Camp
Translated from the French by Gerald Satterwhite.
New York: Anchor Press/Doubleday, 1975, 256 pp. Paper

Betrayed to the Gestapo for organizing a resistance network in Paris, the author and her mother were sent to Ravensbruck in Germany. From her secret notes, interviews with prisoners and examination of camp documents, she reconstructs how the camp operated and the political and pathological ends that it served. The author is an anthropologist, and heads the Graduate Studies Department at the Sorbonne. She was one of the first observers to alert the world to the conditions of the Soviet labor camps. SC

Trepman, Paul
Among Men and Beasts
Translated from the Yiddish by Shoshana Perla and Gertrude Hirschler.
New York: Barnes, 1978, 229 pp.

At the start of the war, the author, a young man in Warsaw, fled to the Ukraine. When the Germans arrived, he returned to Poland. The second part of the memoir concerns life in and around the Warsaw and Rohatyn ghettos, while the last and most substantial section details Trepman's fight to stay alive through six camps. SC

Wells, Leon W.
The Death Brigade
New York: Holocaust Library, 1978 320 pp. Paper. (ADL)

Dr. Wells, a physicist and inventor, recounts his experiences as a young Jew in Lvov, Poland, during the German occupation, focusing on his assignment to the Death Brigade, whose job it was to obliterate traces of mass executions of inmates at Janowska concentration camp. Beyond being a fascinating historical document, this book weaves vivid characters and details into a broad picture that depicts the tragedy of an entire people. Previously published as *The Janowska Road.* SC

Wiesel, Elie
Night
New York: Bantam, 1984, 109 pp. Paper. (ADL)

This brief volume is presented on two levels — that of the author's personal account of his years in concentration camps and the loss of his family, together with his moral dilemma regarding religious faith and conviction. A powerful story about actual events. Highly recommended. Can also be used by slower readers. JSC

In Hiding: Memoirs and Diaries

Brand, Sandra
Between Two Worlds
New York: Shengold, 1982, 126 pp.

Eighteen-year-old Roma, born into a Hasidic family, elopes with an assimilated Jew. the Hasidic Rebbe allows the marriage to stand. The Germans and the Russians occupy the city of Nemirov and the desperate struggle for survival begins. The author of *I Dared To Live* takes us back to the beginning of her story. SC

Brand, Sandra
I Dared to Live
New York: Shengold, 1978, 204 pp.

Story of a survivor who passed as a Gentile in Warsaw and worked with the underground. Ironically, her greatest support came from a German officer increasingly disillusioned with the Nazis and willing to risk his own life to help her survive. JS

Feld, Marilla
I Chose to Live
New York: Woodhill, 1979, 272 pp. Paper.

A young Polish-Jewish dancer passes as a Gentile. She recalls her experiences of hiding in Poland, being taken to Germany as a Polish slave laborer and an eventual happy ending. JS

Flinker, Moshe
Young Moshe's Diary:
The Spiritual Torment of a
Jewish Boy in Nazi Europe
Translated from the Hebrew.
Jerusalem and New York: Yad
Vashem and Board of Jewish
Education, 1965, 126 pp.

A devoutly religious boy from
Holland grapples with the problems
of suffering and divine justice.
Moshe died in Auschwitz. May be
conceptually difficult in parts. SC

Frank, Anne
Diary of a Young Girl
Revised edition.
New York: Doubleday, 1967; Pocket
Books, 1953, 258 pp. Paper.

Touching and optimistic diary of a
young German-Jewish girl who later
died in Bergen-Belsen, written while
in hiding in Amsterdam. Conceptually not difficult. Students can
identify with many of Anne's early
adolescent problems. Includes 64-
page supplement with photographs,
criticism and a brief history of Anne
Frank's life. Also, LP Caedmon (TC
1522) record "Diary of Anne Frank
— abridged Reading by Claire
Bloom." EJS

Friedlander, Saul
When Memory Comes
Translated from the French by
Helen R. Lane.
New York: Farrar, Straus & Giroux,
1979, 192 pp.

In 1939, when he fled
Czechoslovakia with his family, the
author was seven years old. Before
they were taken to the camps his
parents left him in a Catholic
seminary in France. Baptized Paul-
Henri, he trained for the priesthood.
After the war's end he rediscovered
his true identity as a Jew, and in
1948 ran away to Marseilles to
board ship for the nascent state of
Israel. Friedlander, a noted historian
and author of *Pius XII and the Third
Reich* and *Kurt Gerstein: The
Ambiguity of Good,* writes a remarkable and poignant memoir which
deals with past and present.
SC

Joffo, Joseph
A Bag of Marbles
Translated from the French by Mar-
tin Sokolinsky.
New York: Bantam Books, 1977,
243 pp. Paper.

A true story of two Jewish ten-year-
old French school boys during
World War II and how they cope
with anti-Semitism, Nazis and the
dramatic changes in their lives.
JS

Lind, Jakov
Counting My Steps
New York: Macmillan, 1969,
223 pp.

The autobiography of an Austrian-
Jewish writer. (*Soul of Wood and
Other Stories,* New York, Grove,
1965, 190 pp.) Recounts his years
of hiding and fleeing from the
Nazis. SC

Reiss, Johanna
The Upstairs Room
New York: Harper & Row, 1972;
Bantam, 1973, 176 pp. Paper.

True story of the survival of two
Dutch Jewish girls hidden in a
farmhouse throughout the years of
the Nazi occupation. A Newbery
Medal Book. EJ

Tec, Nechama
**Dry Tears: The Story of
a Lost Childhood**
Westport, Conn: Wildcat Publ.,
1982, 216 pp.; Oxford University,
1984, Reprinted with new Epilogue,
242 pp.

Before the war Lublin had a Jewish
population of over 40,000. After the
war a little over one hundred Jews
returned. One of them was
Nechama Tec who was eight years
old when the war started and Lublin
was occupied. She tells how her
parents managed to have the family
"pass" as Christians; of the Polish
Catholics who sheltered them —but
who, after the war, were ashamed of
having done so. Written with res-
traint. The author is now a professor of sociology in Connecticut.
JSC

Weinstein, Frida Scheps
**A Hidden Childhood: A
Jewish Child's Sanctuary in
a French Convent, 1942-1945**
New York: Hill and Wang, 1985,
151 pp. Cloth.

The author describes her extraordinary experiences as a young
Jewish child who was sheltered
from persecution by the Catholic
Church. With great sensitivity, she
recounts the conflict she felt as a
child about her Jewish identity.
EJSC

Zar, Rose with Eric Kimmel
In the Mouth of the Wolf
Philadelphia: Jewish Publication
Society of America, 1983,
225 pp.

Hiding among those who would kill
her, nineteen-year-old Rose
manages to survive the Holocaust
in the midst of Nazis and many
anti-Semitic Poles. How she also
maintains her humanity and faith in
God is part of the story she tells.
JS

Zuker-Bujanowska, Liliana
**Liliana's Journal:
Warsaw, 1939-1945**
New York: Dial Press, 1980,
162 pp.

The author was a young girl from a
fairly assimilated well-to-do family
in a town near Warsaw, when the
Nazis invaded Poland. After the
family was trapped in the Warsaw
Ghetto, her father spirited her out
to Polish Gentiles on the "Aryan"
side. In 1943, she married a member of the Polish underground and
was widowed the year after. She
wrote this memoir in 1946, but
only recently translated it into
English. JSC

Art and Poetry

Blatter, Janet and Sybil Milton
Art of the Holocaust
New York: Rutledge Press, 1981,
272 pp.
Preface by Irving Howe, historical
introduction by Henry Friedlander.

An art book that is also a document, this volume includes more
than 350 art works – scores in
color – created in ghettos, concentration camps and in hiding by victims of the Nazis. The essays and
chapter introductions plus
biographical information on each
artist represented place these
works and their creators in historical and esthetic context. Some of
the pieces are moving, some are
delightful, some beautiful, some the
work of incredibly talented artists.
All are affirmations of the durability
and the insistence of the creative
human spirit. JSC

*Firster, Richard and Nora Levin,
editors*
**The Living Witness:
Art in the Concentration Camps**
Philadelphia: Museum of American
Jewish History, 1978,
48 pp. Paper.

A catalog based on an exhibit prepared by Mary Costanza. The work
of 15 artists of the Holocaust.
JSC

Green, Gerald
The Artists of Terezin
New York: Schocken, 1979,
191 pp. Paper.

More than 100 drawings and paintings with an essay by the author of
the television program "Holocaust."
JSC

Grossman, Mendel
With a Camera in the Ghetto
New York: Schocken, 1977,
107 pp.

Compelling photos of everyday life
in the Lodz Ghetto, recording the
miseries as well as the resistance
and dignity of the inhabitants. This
book represents a fraction of
Grossman's original 10,000
negatives, which survived World War
II and were brought to Israel only to
be lost during the War of Independence. JSC

Gurdus, Luba Krugman
**Painful Echoes. . . Poems of the
Holocaust from the Diary of
Luba Krugman Gurdus**
New York: Holocaust Library, 1985,
80 pp. Paper.
Introduction by Martin Gilbert.

More than a score of poems selec-
ted from the diary kept by Luba
Gurdus during her periods of hiding.
The poems appear in their original

Polish and in English translation. The volume also includes 58 black-and-white drawings by the author, who is an artist.

A moving collection. Recommended for all ages and for courses in poetry, the arts, and Holocaust studies. JSC

Kalisch, Shoshana and Meistev, Barbara
Yes, We Sang: Songs of the Ghettos and Concentration Camps
New York: Harper and Row, 1985, 160 pp. Cloth.

Contains music and words of 25 songs. Each song is introduced with information about the composer and/or the setting in which each song originated — camps, ghettos, etc. The author is a survivor of Auschwitz. EJSC

Kantor, Alfred
The Book of Alfred Kantor
New York: McGraw-Hill, 1971.

Introduction by John Wykert. The personal story of the author-artist of the 127 sketches of life done as an inmate in Terezin, Auschwitz and Schwarzheide. JSC

Mlotek, Eleanor and Gottlieb, Malke (compilers)
We Are Here: Songs of the Holocaust
New York: Hippocrene Books and Workmen's Circle, 1985, 104 pp. Paper.

Forty songs, with texts in Yiddish and in English. Includes many that are not well-known. Singable translations by Roslyn Bresnick-Perry. The bibliography and the notes about the songs are in Yiddish. Black-and-white illustrations by Tsirl Waletsky. Foreword by Elie Wiesel. EJSC

Sachs, Nelly
O The Chimneys: Selected Poems
Translated from the German by several translators.
New York: Farrar, Straus & Giroux, 1967, 387 pp.; also paper; Philadelphia: Jewish Publication Society, 1968.

The author, a winner of the Nobel Prize for literature in 1966, was a German Jew who escaped to Sweden in 1940. "The chimneys" refer to the crematoriums. SC

Sachs, Nelly
The Seeker and Other Poems
Translated from the German by Ruth and Matthew Mead and Michael Hamburger.
New York: Farrar, Straus & Giroux, 1970, 399 pp.

Poems expressing the Jewish flight from Nazi terror and memorials to her "6,000,000 brothers and sisters" who perished in the Holocaust. SC

Spiritual Resistance: Art from Concentration Camps, 1940-45
Philadelphia: Jewish Publication Society, 1981, 240 pp.; Union of American Hebrew Congregations, 1978, 72 pp. Paper.

More than 100 works by 49 artists. Their works, from the collection of the Ghetto Fighters' House in Israel, were exhibited at museums in New York, Los Angeles, Baltimore, Cambridge, Newark, Louisville and Chicago. Includes essays by Lucy Dawidowicz and Tom Freudenheim, Director of the Baltimore Museum of Art. JSC

Toll, Nelly
Without Surrender:
Art of the Holocaust
Philadelphia: Running Press, 1978, 109 pp. Paper.

Nelly Toll, survivor and artist, has collected some 80 paintings and drawings, almost all of which were done in the camps and ghettos. She provides information about many of the artists and an essay on art of the Holocaust.
J (with discretion) SC

✓ *Volavkova, H., editor*
I Never Saw Another Butterfly: Children's Drawings & Poems from Terezin Concentration Camp, 1942-1944
Translated from the Czech by Jeanne Nemcova. New York: Schocken, 80 pp. Paper. (ADL)

A must for all collections. EJS

Fiction

✓ *Appelfeld, Aharon*
Tzili: The Story of a Life
Translated from the Hebrew by Dalya Bilu
New York: Dutton, 1983, 185 pp.

Reminiscent of a parable, this novel tells the story of a poor, stupid Jewish girl, left behind as her family flees, yet one who unwittingly manages to survive the Holocaust in the company of the local Polish peasants. The sparse narrative is full of anguish, yet not totally defeating. *Tzili* completes Appelfeld's trilogy: *Badenheim 1939,* and *The Age of Wonders.* JSC

Borowski, Tadeusz
This Way for The Gas, Ladies and Gentlemen
Translated from the Polish.
New York: Penguin, 1976, 160 pp. Paper.

A Polish poet's short stories, haunting in their simplicity, based on his experiences in Auschwitz. A slim but powerful volume. For more mature students. SC

✓ *Demetz, Hana*
The House on Prague Street
New York: G.K. Hall, 1980, 186 pp. (large print).

A deceptively simple autobiographical novel provides a glimpse of an assimilated and well-to-do Czechoslovakian Jewish family. The author, whose father was a German citizen, was an adolescent when the war brought disintegration and death. A sense of innocence pervades the book. JSC

Epstein, Leslie
King of the Jews
New York: Avon, 1980,
350 pp. Paper.

Macabre and controversial novel of a ghetto in Poland and the head of the Judenrat, the Nazi-imposed Jewish town council. Loosely based on the Lodz Ghetto and Chaim Rumkowski, the egomaniacal Judenrat chairman. Raises important questions. SC

Forman, James
The Survivor
New York: Farrar, Straus & Giroux, 1976, 288 pp.

Abraham Ullman is a Dutch-Jewish physician who refuses to believe that the Nazi invasion will affect the life of his family – and when he does it is too late. His brother and daughter join the underground, his father commits suicide and he, his wife, their twin teenage sons David and Saul, and the youngest child, Rachel, go into hiding. An absorbing story. JS

David Olere, *Forced Labor, Building a Tunnel, 1945*

Green, Gerald
Holocaust
New York: Bantam, 1978,
408 pp.

The saga of a gentle and compassionate Jewish physician and his family from 1935 to 1945, all of whom are in different ways brutalized by the Nazi terror. Parallel to this family's tragic history runs the story of an ambitious young German lawyer who, prodded by his even more ambitious wife, joins the SS and becomes an aide to the chief planner of the annihilation of the Jews. Based on the nine and-one-half-hour NBC-TV docudrama. JS

Hersey, John
The Wall
New York: Knopf, 1950.

Truth through fiction. A monumental work concerning the creation of the Warsaw Ghetto, the building of the "Wall" around it, the uprising and the destruction of the ghetto. Gripping. (See also Millard Lampell's dramatization, Knopf, 1961.)
SC

Keneally, Thomas
Schindler's List
New York: Simon & Schuster, 1982,
400 pp.; Penguin, 1983, paper.

The technique of a novel is used to
tell this true story of Oskar Schindler, a German who owned a factory outside Cracow where
concentration camp inmates were
sent to work. He entertained (and
provided entertainment for) Nazi
officials, was something of a roué
— and secretly sheltered and saved
more than a thousand Jews within
the factory confines. Based on
interviews with 50 Schindler survivors (Schindler's Jews) worldwide;
supplemented by written and other
documentary material. Fascinating.
Also raises interesting questions
about the nature of altruists. JSC

 Kosinski, Jerzy
The Painted Bird
Second edition.
New York: Modern Library, 1982;
Bantam, 1972, 224 pp. Paper.

Novel focusing on a young boy
abandoned by his parents in Eastern Europe during World War II and
mistakenly thought to be a Jew or
Gypsy. His adolescent innocence
encounters terror and brutality. The
author delves into the Nazi mentality. For mature readers. Conceptually very difficult for ninth- and
tenth-grade students. Juniors and
seniors may have some difficulty
also. Teachers should use caution
and read it before using. SC

Kuznetsov, Anatoli
**Babi Yar: A Document in the
Form of a Novel**
Uncensored edition. Translated
from the Russian by David Floyd.
Cambridge: Robert Bentley, 1979
reprint; Washington Square Press/
Simon & Schuster, 1982,
416 pp. Paper.

From a Russian boy's look at the
massacre of Jews near Kiev by the
Nazis. To this day, the Soviet Union
refuses to acknowledge that Jews
were slaughtered there, referring to
them only as Soviet citizens. The
writer defected to the West. SC

Lustig, Arnost
**Darkness Casts
No Shadows**
Translated from the Czech by
Jeanne Nevmcova.
Washington, DC: Inscape, 1976,
144 pp.; Avon, 1976, 173 pp.
Paper.

Two adolescent boys escape from a
concentration-camp-bound train
and run for freedom. This novel
records their "adventures." Made
into a feature film *Diamonds in the
Night* (see below).

Lustig, Arnost
Night and Hope
Translated from the Czech by
George Theiner.
Washington, DC: Inscape, 1976,
206 pp.; Avon, 1976, 219 pp.
Paper.

Powerful vignettes describing the

world where the author came of age – Terezin, showing us the most dignified and the most degrading aspects of human nature reacting to intractable circumstances. Based on actual records of the administrative procedure deployed in the ghetto-camp by the Third Reich. See film, *Transport From Paradise,* below. SC

Lustig, Arnost
A Prayer for Katerina Horovitzova
Translated from the Czech by Jeanne Nevmcova.
New York: Avon, 1975, 191 pp. Paper.

Twenty American Jewish businessmen and a young girl are caught in a macabre game of self-deception master minded by the Nazis and end up in a death camp. Devastating. SC

Orlev, Uri
The Island on Bird Street
Translated from the Hebrew by Hillel Halkin.
Boston: Houghton, Mifflin, 1984, 162 pp.

Forced to take refuge in an abandoned building in the Warsaw Ghetto, eleven-year-old Alex learns how to survive on his own. But Alex has hope because he is waiting for his father. The author draws on his own experiences for this novel. Winner of several awards including the prestigious Mildred L. Batchelder Award, which honors one book each

year for the outstanding example of books published originally in a foreign country and foreign language. EJ

Orlev, Uri
The Lead Soldier
Translated from the Hebrew by Hillel Halkin.
New York: Taplinger, 1980, 234 pp.

A semi-autobiographical novel of a young boy's journey from a suburb of Warsaw to the Ghetto to Bergen-Belsen. Yurik and his kid brother Kazik transmute the life and death around them into children's games. "A small master piece." Jewish Chronicle. JSC

Schaeffer, Susan Fromberg
Anya
New York: Bard/Avon, 1975, 616 pp. Paper.

A gripping novel of a young woman from a well-to-do cultured family in Vilna, growing up in the 20's and 30's, through experiences in the ghetto, camps, and after the war. SC

Schwarz-Bart, Andre
Last of the Just
Translated from the French by Stephen Becker.
Cambridge: Robert Bentley, 1981; Atheneum, 1977, 374 pp. Paper.

The story of Ernie Levy, last of a hereditary line of the 36 righteous men for whose sake God allows the world to continue. The young German-Jewish boy takes upon himself the suffering of others. Winner of France's Goncourt Prize for Literature. Excerpt in *Out of the Whirlwind.* (see above.) SC

Siegal, Aranka
Upon the Head of the Goat: A Childhood in Hungary, 1939-1944
New York: Farrar, Straus & Giroux, 1981, 213 pp.; also paper, 1981, 192 pp.

A fictionalized memoir of the author's and her family's heroic responses to the slow destruction of the Jewish community in Hitler-dominated Hungary. Winner of the Janusz Korczak and Newbery Awards. JS

Steiner, Jean-Francois
Treblinka
Translated from the French by Helen Weaver.
New York: New American Library, 1979, 304 pp. Paper. (ADL)

Powerful novel about the Treblinka extermination camp and a revolt by the prisoners. Intended to dispel the notion that all victims marched unresisting to their death. May be difficult for some grades. Conceptually basic. SC

Uris, Leon
QB VII
New York: Doubleday, 1972, 564 pp.; Bantam. Paper.

Novel about a libel suit by a doctor against a New York writer who claims the physician participated in inhuman experiments on patients in his charge while he worked in a concentration camp. The full story of what happened during the war years is brought out during testimony at the trial. Film version stars Ben Gazzara, Jack Hawkins, Anthony Quayle. SC

Uris, Leon
Mila 18
New York: Doubleday, 1961, 539 pp.; Bantam, 1981, 576 pp. Paper.

A street in the Warsaw Ghetto where the Jews made their last stand. SC

Wiesel, Elie
The Gates of the Forest
Translated from the French by Frances Frenaye.
New York: Schocken, 1982, 240 pp. Paper.

A young Hungarian Jew escapes to the forest during the Nazi occupation, masquerades as a mute in another village and joins the Jewish partisans. Wiesel probes the demonological dimension of the Holocaust and blends its experiences with stories of past and present Jewish travail. SC

AUDIO-VISUAL

Border Street
110 minutes/black-and-white/
feature film/ JWB Lecture Bureau

Polish with English subtitles

Fictionalization of Warsaw's Jews
and non-Jews during the Nazi
occupation. Revolves around a
group of Jewish and non-Jewish
youngsters who, prior to the war,
lived and played on the same
street. Ends with the battle of the
Warsaw Ghetto. JSC

Diamonds of the Night
70 minutes/black-and-white/feature
film/Czech with English
subtitles/Icarus

Based on the novel *Darkness Casts
No Shadows,* by Arnost Lustig (see
above). Explores the subconscious
minds of two Jewish teenage boys
who escape from a concentration-
camp-bound death transport. With
a minimum of dialogue the film
records their escape journey. It
does not rely on the obvious
horrors of war; no one kicks or
beats the boys or tortures them.
Rather, the film studies the boys,
isolated on the outer edge of exis-
tence, overwhelmed by fear and
physical exhaustion, humiliated and
near despair, and simply finds they
will not give up their desperate fight
for life. Called "blackly lyrical."
SC

The Diary of Anne Frank
180 minutes/black-and-white/
Feature film/Jewish Media
Service/JWB

Based on the book (see above). JS

The Fifth Horseman Is Fear
100 minutes/16 mm/black-and-
white.
Available in subtitled and dubbed
versions/Audio Brandon

A Jewish doctor caught in the web
of Nazi horror. A Czech film
depicting the Nazi takeover of
Prague. SC

A Field of Buttercups
30 minutes/black-and-white/
National Academy

Dramatization of the life and work
of Dr. Janusz Korczak, who follows
the 200 orphans in his charge to
the gas chambers — although he
himself has an opportunity to leave
in safety. See Korczak's *Ghetto
Diary,* above. S

The Garden of the Finzi-Continis
103 minutes/16 mm/color/
Cinema Five

The decline and fall of Italian Jewry
through the life of one family in
Ferrara. Directed by Vittorio de Sica.
Based on the novel by Giorgio
Bassani (Harvest, 1977. Paper).
SC

I Never Saw Another Butterfly
30 minutes/kinescope/black-and-white/feature/National Academy

For twenty years, "Anya," one of the 100 children who survived the Terezin concentration camp, repressed her experiences. Her own child knows nothing of her past. Urged by her husband, "Anya" returns to Terezin and relives those years. Includes poetry and drawings of children at the camp gathered in the book *I Never Saw Another Butterfly* (see above). S

In the Beginning
30 minutes/kinescope/black-and-white/National Academy

The story of Noah, a teacher trapped in the Warsaw Ghetto with a few remaining Jews, who insists on celebrating the festival of Simhat Torah. Eternal Light production. JS

Jacob the Liar
95 minutes/color/feature film (German with English subtitles) Audio-Brandon/JWB Lecture Bureau

Hope of salvation is kept alive in the hearts of the Jews in the ghetto as they await deportation. Based on the novel by Jurek Becker. Powerful and beautiful. SC

Kapo
116 minutes/black-and-white/ JWB Lecture Bureau

A study of hope and humiliation in Nazi slave labor camps. Focuses on a 14-year-old Jewish girl who learns to save herself through a series of moral compromises. Assuming the identity of a French thief, she sleeps with non-officers and becomes a "Kapo," a prisoner who oversees — often brutally — other prisoners. Among the questions it raises: What price survival? SC

The Last Rabbi
30 minutes/kinescope/black-and-white/National Academy

Based on actual documents left by Jews in the Warsaw Ghetto, this Eternal Light drama relates how the last surviving rabbi refused to accept an opportunity to escape death at the hands of the Nazis. S

The Legacy of Anne Frank
30 minutes/black-and-white or color/National Academy

Filmed in Holland. Shots of youngsters today at the school Anne went to and interviews with her teachers juxtaposed with the story of Anne Frank, her family and Dutch Jewry, Dutch resistance and Westerbork internment camp. JS

Music of Auschwitz
16 minutes/color/not cleared for TV/ADL

Fanya Fenelon tells the story of her

imprisonment in Paris as a member of the French underground and — because she was Jewish — her deportation to Auschwitz. As a member of the orchestra, Fenelon played march cadences by day for the prisoners on their way to the gas chambers and waltz tempos at night for the entertainment of the Nazi guards. Originally a segment for "60 Minutes." See her memoir *Playing for Time*, above. SC

Night and Fog
31 minutes/color/French narration with English subtitles/not cleared for TV/ADL

A brilliant film on the concentration camp world in all its piercing and compelling truth, by one of the foremost French directors, Alain Resnais. Resnais takes his cameras to major concentration camps of the Nazi era, now hauntingly barren and innocent, and over these scenes superimposes historic footage evoking the dreadful past. A classic. SC

Nightmare: The Immigration of Joachim and Rachael
24 minutes/color/Multimedia/ ADL/Jewish Media Service

A dramatic reenactment of two children struggling to escape from the Warsaw Ghetto. EJ

The Shop on Main Street
128 minutes/black-and-white/ feature film/Jewish Media Service/ JWB/Audio-Brandon/Czech with English subtitles

A haunting tragicomedy set during the early days of the Nazi occupation of Czechoslovakia. With Ida Kaminska. In a small Slovak town, an itinerant carpenter is appointed by his brother-in-law, a Nazi collaborator, as the Aryan controller of the worthless button-shop of an old, deaf Jewish woman. Instead of hidden riches, he finds a good human being. During a roundup of Jews, he fails her and himself. Based on the novel by Ladislaw Grossman, Doubleday, 1970. SC

Halina Olomucki, *Women in Birkenau, 1945*

Stars

94 minutes/black-and-white/
JWB Lecture Bureau/feature film

A German sergeant and would-be artist oversees Bulgarian workers, some of whom are partisans. He meets a young Greek Jew on her way to Auschwitz. (Note that the Bulgarian government did not allow its Jewish citizens to be deported but acquiesced to the Nazis regarding foreign Jews.) Reluctantly at first, he becomes involved in helping the partisans in trying to save the girl. Moving. Cannes Festival award winner. SC

Sweet Light in a Dark Room

93 minutes/black-and-white/feature film/JWB Lecture Bureau/Czech with English titles

Originally titled "Romeo, Juliet and Darkness," the film explores human kindness, love, suspicion and tragedy — the face of war and destruction, as a young Aryan student vainly attempts to save a Jewish girl from death. SC

Transport From Paradise

94 minutes/black-and-white/feature film/Czech and German with English subtitles/Icarus

Based on *Night and Hope* by Arnost Lustig (see above), the film explores the nightmarish interaction between Jews and the meticulous efficiency of the Nazi program for extermination. Searing. SC

The Two of Us

86 minutes/black-and-white/
dubbed version/Swank

A young Jewish boy from Paris is saved from deportation and sent to live with an elderly French farm couple. The farmer does not like Jews. The man and boy learn about life and each other in a tender and compassionate film. Directed by Claude Berri and starring Michel Simon. EJS

The Upstairs Room

2 strips/color/cassette or record/
teacher's guide/Social Studies
School Service

Based on the memoir by Johanna Reiss (see above). Original drawings, first-person narrative. For younger children. EJ

Warsaw Ghetto: Holocaust and Resistance

Filmstrip/130 frames/19 minutes/
black-and-white/cassette/
Jewish Labor Committee and Social Studies School Service

Based upon the recollections of survivors of the Warsaw Ghetto and photographs and documents hidden by the resistance fighters. Focusing on life within the Ghetto under the Nazi regime, the program shows the reactions to oppression and the final efforts against the German occupation. Narrated by Theodore Bikel. JS

Warsaw Ghetto
51 minutes/black-and-white/ADL

Film footage taken from 1940 to 1943 of the mile-square, walled-off Warsaw Ghetto. Assembled over a period of twenty years, pictures of life and death in the Ghetto were taken by cameramen of the German army, the SS and the Gestapo, many for the private albums of Heinrich Himmler, Gestapo chief. The documentary shows the frightened, bewildered Jews entering the Ghetto area; the horrors of disease, hunger, and systematic deportations to death camps; and finally the heroic uprising that preceded the annihilation and ultimate silence in the Ghetto. Produced by BBC-TV. Guide available. SC

The Witnesses
82 minutes/black-and-white/
French with English subtitles/
JWB Lecture Bureau

A French documentary by the team responsible for *To Die in Madrid*. Contains newsreel footage of the Warsaw Ghetto taken by the Germans between 1940 and 1943, as in BBC's "Warsaw Ghetto" (minus the grotesque eating scenes), plus much not seen before. Most of the narrative is from memoirs and documents. Powerful. SC

Collaboration and Indifference

When all allowances have been made, when all mitigating circumstances have been accorded, it is still true that few come out of the story unblemished.

Walter Laqueur
The Terrible Secret

PUBLICATIONS

Abella, Irving M. and Harold Troper
None is Too Many: Canada and the Jews of Europe, 1933-1948
New York: Random House, 1983, 336 pp.

The authors argue that Canadian immigration policies during World War II were formulated by anti-Semites and resulted in under-populated Canada's acceptance of only 5000 Jews from 1933-1945 and only 8000 more until 1948. The painstaking detail is occasionally repetitious, though this does not mar the scholarship. C

Elon, Amos
Timetable
Garden City, NY: Doubleday, 1980, 349 pp.

In May 1944, Eichmann offered to release Hungarian Jews scheduled for deportation and death in exchange for trucks, coffee, soap. He sent Joel Brand, a Jew active in resistance, to neutral Turkey to deliver the offer. Was it real? Why was it made? How should and did the British, the Americans, the Russians and the Jews respond? Lord Moyne, the British Minister Resident in Cairo, is reported to have said: "A million Jews! Whatever would we do with them?" Elon has told this true and chilling story in the form of a novel, perhaps to enhance its readability. (For a brief recounting which includes information not available to Elon, see Bernard Wasserstein, *Britain and the Jews of Europe 1939-1945,* pp. 249-63, below.) JSC

Feingold, Henry L.
The Politics of Rescue:
The Roosevelt Administration and the Holocaust, 1938-1945
Updated and expanded edition.
New York: Holocaust Library, 1980, 432 pp. Paper. (ADL)

Scholarly history of the failure of

the United States to rescue European Jewry. Also probes the futility of intervention by official American Jewish agencies. SC

Hochhuth, Rolf
The Deputy
Translated from the German by Richard Winston and Clara Winston. New York: Grove Press, 1964, 352 pp. Paper.

Full English translation and 65 pages of historical notes on the controversial seven-hour play about the role of Pope Pius XII during Hitler's annihilation of six million European Jews. SC

Laqueur, Walter
The Terrible Secret:
The Suppression of the Truth about Hitler's "Final Solution"
Boston: Little, Brown, 1980, 262 pp.; Penguin, paper. (ADL, paper)

When did information about the genocide first become known to Jews and non-Jews? Through what channels was this information transmitted? What was the reaction of those who received word of the slaughter?

According to Laqueur, word started to spread soon after extermination began. But there is no easy, straightforward answer to the wider question of why there was a failure to read correctly the signs in 1941, of why so many individuals and governments actually chose to deny

the reality of genocide when faced with incontrovertible evidence. "In some cases the motives were creditable, in others damnable. In some instances moral categories are simply not applicable, and there were also cases which defy understanding to this day." A probing and disturbing work. SC

Morley, John F.
Vatican Diplomacy and the Jews During the Holocaust 1939-1943
New York: KTAV, 1980
327 pp. (ADL)

A country-by-country analysis based on previously unpublished materials from the Vatican archives. Except for a few localized instances the Pope followed a neutral course, writes the author, a Roman Catholic priest-scholar, because the Vatican apparently felt that maintaining diplomatic relations with the occupied nations was a more primary concern. C

Morse, Arthur D.
While Six Million Died:
A Chronicle of American Apathy
New York: Overlook, 1983, 432 pp.

"This volume concentrates on the bystanders." The story of the deliberate obstructions placed by the U.S.A. and Britain in the way of attempts to rescue European Jews from Hitler's Final Solution. The author uses contemporary newspapers and government documents and shows that not only were specific opportunities for rescue ignored, but over 1,000,000 U.S. immigration quota openings were unfilled between 1933 and 1943. SC

Penkower, Monty Noam
The Jews Were Expendable: Free World Diplomacy and the Holocaust
Urbana: University of Illinois Press, 1983, 302 pp. Cloth.

Nominated for a National Jewish Book Award, this book provides an overview of the free world's tragic failure to respond decisively to the Holocaust. In nine semi-independent essays Penkower reconstructs various episodes in the history of the diplomacy of the Holocaust — among them, the Bermuda conference in April 1943 and the creation of the U.S. War Refugee Board in January 1944. Among Penkower's most disturbing and compelling revelations is the story of how Hitler's scheme to destroy the Jewish people finally came to light. C

Ross, Robert W.
So It Was True: The American Protestant Press and the Nazi Persecution of the Jews
Minneapolis: University of Minnesota Press, 1980, 374 pp. Also paper. (ADL, paper)

Examines Protestant religious

periodicals that were regularly circulated at the parish level between 1933 and 1945, to determine what information was given regarding the plight of the Jews under the Nazis. Questions why the American church was either silent during the war years, or protested ineffectively and too late. C

Thomas, Gordon and Max Morgan Witts
Voyage of the Damned
New York: Stein and Day, 1974, 317 pp.

Hour-by-hour reconstruction of the voyage of the St. Louis, the German luxury liner that sailed from Hamburg to Cuba in May 1939 and was refused entry by the Cubans — as well as by other nations. Focuses on corruption, manipulation, indifference, and desperation. JS

Wasserstein, Bernard
Britain and the Jews of Europe 1939-1945
New York: Oxford University Press, 1979, 389 pp.

Based on diplomatic notes, minutes of meetings, diaries, private letters — most of which were only recently released by the British Government. "The problems discussed in this book were, for the Jews of Europe, a matter of life and death; they were of only secondary importance in the eyes of the British Government. Yet the fundamental question arises...Was Britain's wartime policy towards the Jewish problem the only possible one compatible with the overriding end of victory." An important and disturbing study. SC

Wyman, David
The Abandonment of the Jews: America and the Holocaust, 1941-1945
New York: Pantheon, 1984, 444 pp.

An important and devastating study of this nation's limited response, lack of response and negative response to Europe's Jews during World War II. A meticulously documented report, carefully and painfully analyzed, which indicts our government and almost every segment of our society. Winner of the National Jewish Book Award. C

AUDIO-VISUAL

Lacombe, Lucien
137 minutes/color/French with English subtitles/Films Incorporated/JWB Lecture Bureau

Chronicles a peasant boy's period of adolescence in Nazi-occupied France. "The exploitation of individual ambition, weakness, prejudice and frustration by a demonic system in need of accomplices, be they the active or the passive variety. We are confronted with self-servicing rationalizations used by the accomplices, men, women and children, in all walks of life — to justify their seduction into barbarity." Medium, Nov.-Dec. 1974. SC

The Sorrow and the Pity
260 minutes/black-and-white/ French with English subtitles/ Cinema Five

An unrelenting documentary about collaboration and resistance during the German occupation of France. By Marcel Ophuls. SC

Voyage of the Damned
158 minutes/color/Films Inc./ JWB Lecture Bureau

The story of the 937 German-Jewish refugees aboard the luxury liner St. Louis who sailed to Cuba in 1939 but were forcibly returned to Europe as World War II was about to begin. Based on the book by Thomas and Witts (see above). JSC

Resistance and Rescue

I shall not go to slave labor; I shall not join any workers' group! The intention of the Nazi Satan is not only to enslave the body; his main goal is to subjugate the soul. We shall not submit. We give up the food rations. We shall starve, but will not be moved. We shall find somehow some way of getting something to eat... We shall oppose the decrees of the Satan.

A Hasid

PUBLICATIONS

Ainsztein, Reuben
The Warsaw Ghetto Revolt
New York: Holocaust Library, 1979, 238 pp. Paper. (ADL)

An account by an authority on Jewish resistance in Eastern Europe. SC

Anger, Per
With Raoul Wallenberg in Budapest: Memories of the War Years in Hungary
Translated from the Swedish by David Mel Paul and Margareta Paul.
New York: Holocaust Library, 1981, 192 pp. Also paper. (ADL, also paper)

Raoul Wallenberg was Secretary of the Swedish Legation in Budapest in 1944. He was responsible for saving about 25,000 Jews directly and another 70,000 indirectly. Per Anger, a close associate of Wallenberg, writes of these events, of Wallenberg's arrest by the Russians and his subsequent disappearance. Illustrated. JSC

Arad, Yitzhak
The Partisan: From the Valley of Death to Mount Zion
New York: Holocaust Library, 1979, 288 pp., 56 photographs. Also paper. (ADL, also paper)

Thirteen years old when the Germans overran Warsaw, the author escaped to the Soviet-occupied part of Poland. When the Nazis came two years later, he became a partisan in the Lithuanian forests. After the war he immigrated to Palestine and was active in Israel's War of Independence. Dr. Arad currently serves as Chairman of the Directorate of Yad Vashem in Jerusalem. SC

Bartoszewski, Wladyslaw, in collaboration with Zofia Lewin
The Samaritans: Heroes of the Holocaust
Boston: Twayne, 1970, 442 pp.

"Accounts of the martyrdom of Poland's Jews tend to emphasize their suffering at the hands of blackmailers and informers, the 'blue police' and other scum. Less is written, on the other hand, about the thousands of Poles who risked their lives to save the Jews. The flotsam and jetsam on the surface of a turbulent river is more visible than the pure stream running underneath, but that stream existed" (Adolph Berman, member of the Jewish Underground in Poland). Accounts of Poles from all walks of life who helped the Jews. SC

Bauer, Yehuda
They Chose Life: Jewish Resistance in the Holocaust
New York: American Jewish Committee, 1973, 64 pp. Paper.

Brief overview of the history of the Holocaust, the Jewish Councils and various types of resistance. Illustrated. JSC

✓ *Benchley, Nathaniel*
Bright Candles
New York: Harper and Row, 1974, 256 pp.

Novel about a 16-year-old Danish boy who becomes part of a resistance group, in opposition to his parents who believe that cooperation is the safest course. EJS

✓ *Bishop, Claire Huchet*
Twenty and Ten
New York: Peter Smith, 1984; Viking/Penguin, 1978, 76 pp. Paper.

Twenty French children help hide and protect ten Jewish refugee children during the German occupation. Based on a true story. For younger readers. E

Chary, Frederick B.
The Bulgarian Jews and the Final Solution, 1940-44
Pittsburgh: University of Pittsburgh, 1972, 246 pp.

Almost all of Bulgaria's Jewish citizens escaped the Final Solution. Why? The author describes the Bulgarian government's vacillation under pressure between the Allies and the Axis and the interaction between various political groups and individual leaders. He also writes about the fate of Jews deported from Greece through Bulgaria (these were sent to their deaths). As an interesting sideline, the author states that "the association of Fascism with anti-Semitism is not verified by the facts," citing the examples of both Bulgaria and Italy to substantiate his claims. SC

✓ *Cowan, Lori*
Children of the Resistance
New York: Hawthorne Books, 1969;
Archway Paperback, 1971, 229 pp.

Eight accounts, each set in a different country in occupied Europe, of teenagers who played roles in the underground resistance against the Nazis. Writing somewhat stilted but good stories of examples of bravery. J

Eckman, Lester S. and Chaim Lazar
The Jewish Resistance
New York: Shengold, 1977,
282 pp.

An account of the resistance to the Nazis in Lithuania and White Russia during World War II, based on documents and interviews with more than 400 former partisans. Eckman was a child in Vilna during the war; Lazar was a freedom fighter in the Vilna Ghetto. JSC

Elkins, Michael
Forged in Fury
New York: Ballantine, 1971,
312 pp. Paper.

Stories of Jews, survivors of the Holocaust now living in Israel, who formed a secret organization aiming to take vengeance upon the killers of Jews. JS

Flender, Harold
Rescue in Denmark
New York: Holocaust Library, 1980,
280 pp. Paper. (ADL)

An account of the heroism of the Danish people in saving Jews from the Nazis in 1943 — an act which helped mobilize and strengthen the initially weak resistance movement. See also *Act of Faith* (A-V section below). For a more scholarly presentation, see Leni Yahil, *The Rescue of Danish Jewry: Test of a Democracy* (Philadelphia: Jewish Publication Society, 1969).
EJS

✓ *Forman, James*
Ceremony of Innocence
New York: Dell, 1977,
208 pp. Paper.

Novel based on the true story of the "White Rose" — six university students who revolted against the Nazi regime in 1942-1943 and were executed. For documentary accounts, see Hanser, *A Noble Treason* (below), and Inge Scholl, *Students Against Tyranny* (Wesleyan University Press, 1970). JS

Friedman, Philip
**Their Brothers' Keepers:
The Christian Heroes and
Heroines Who Helped the
Oppressed Escape the Nazi
Terror**
New York: Holocaust Library, 1978,
232 pp. Paper. (ADL)

Well-documented and deeply moving. JSC

Gruber, Ruth
Haven: The Unknown Story of a Thousand World War II Refugees
New York: Coward-McCann, 1983, 335 pp.

The author, then a young assistant to Harold L. Ickes, Secretary of the Interior, was sent by the U.S. government to escort refugees from war-torn Italy to Fort Ontario, a former army camp on Lake Ontario. Simply and passionately, she tells of their life in the refugee camp, their struggle to fight deportation, the roles played by the State Department, Eleanor Roosevelt, and Secretary of the Treasury Henry Morgenthau, Jr. JS

Gutman, Yisrael and Ephraim Zuroff
Rescue Attempts During the Holocaust: Proceedings of the Second Yad Vashem International Historical Conference — April, 1974
Jerusalem: Yad Vashem, 1977, 679 pp.

Contents: The Negotiations Between Saly Mayer and the Representatives of the SS in 1944-45; The Rescue Work of the World Jewish Congress During the Nazi Period; The International Red Cross and its Policy vis-a-vis the Jews in the Ghettos and Concentration Camps in Nazi-Occupied Europe; Roosevelt and the Resettlement Question; British Policy on Immigration to Palestine During World War II; The British Government and the Fate of Hungarian Jewry in 1944; The Attitude of the Soviet Union to the Rescue of Jews; The Problem of the Rescue of German Jewry During the Years 1933-1939; The Emigration of Jews from Worms (November 1938-October 1941); Rescue in Lithuania During the Nazi Occupation; Jewish Family Camps in the Forests — An Original Means of Rescue; The Activities of the Council for Aid to Jews ("Zegota") in Occupied Poland; The Attitude of the Poles to the Mass Deportations of Jews from the Warsaw Ghetto in the Summer of 1942; The Role of the Czech and Slovak Jewish Leadership in the Field of Rescue Work; The Activities of the Jewish Agency Delegation in Istanbul in 1943; The Rescue of Jews in the Italian Zone of Occupied Croatia; The Position of the Jews in Occupied Holland during World War II; The Zionist Underground in Holland and France and the Escape to Spain; Jewish Rescue Activities in Belgium and France; The Uniqueness of the Rescue of Danish Jewry; The "Righteous Among the Nations" and their Part in the Rescue of Jews. SC

Gutman, Yisrael
The Jews of Warsaw, 1939-1943: Ghetto, Underground, Revolt
Translated from the Hebrew by Ina Friedman
Bloomington, IN: Indiana University Press, 1982, 487 pp.

A meticulously researched examination of the Jewish community in Warsaw and of the intellectual and psychological means which were adapted by that community in order to cope with Nazi persecution. Gutman speaks as both participant and historian. Assumes knowledge of the larger political and diplomatic context. SC

Hallie, Phillip
**Lest Innocent Blood be Shed:
The Story of the Village
of Le Chambon and How
Goodness Happened There**
New York: Harper & Row, 1979, 304 pp. (ADL)

In full view of the Vichy government and a nearby division of Nazi SS, this Protestant village in southern France, led by its clergy, saved thousands of Jews from death. Based on the testimony of the villagers. Illustrated. SC

Hanser, Richard
**A Noble Treason:
The Revolt of the Munich
Students Against Hitler**
New York: Putnam, 1979, 319 pp.

Six university students gradually grow to understand what National Socialism is all about. They form the "White Rose" and openly fight the regime. All were killed by the Nazis. Based on documents and interviews.
SC

Hellman, Peter
Avenue of the Righteous
New York: Atheneum, 1980, 267 pp. Bantam. Paper.

Moving portraits of Christians who saved Jews: a Dutch carpenter and his daughter, a Belgian cleaning woman and her husband, a French woman — mistress of a Belgian doctor, a French haberdasher and a Polish woman whose husband was killed by the Nazis. Has the elements of a TV Thriller. JSC

Huneke, Douglas K.
The Moses of Rovno
New York: Dodd, Mead, 1985, 228 pp. Cloth.

Robert McAfee Brown, Professor of Theology and Ethics, Pacific School of Religion at Berkeley says it best: "This book combines a story of high moral passion with all the excitement of a spy thriller. Fritz Graebe, who as a non-Jew risked his life repeatedly during World War II to save Jews from Hitler's firing squads and death camps, was also an exceedingly astute and clever man who time and again outwitted the Nazis at their own game. . . As we face our own moral dilemmas, we can only hope that some of Fritz Graebe's courage rubs off on us." The author is a Presbyterian minister in California. There is a foreword by Rabbi Harold M. Schulweis, founder of the Center for the Study of Righteous Acts. SC

Kluger, Ruth and Peggy Mann
The Last Escape:
The Launching of
the Largest Secret
Rescue Movement of All Times
Garden City: Doubleday, 1973, ix +
518 pp.; Pinnacle Books, 1978.
Paper.

The true story of the "illegal
immigration" movement and its
efforts to rescue Jews from Europe.
Exciting action story moves across
the Balkans to Istanbul and conveys
a vivid picture of life in that period.
Includes the story of an outstanding
heroine. JCS
Adaptions of this book include: *The
Secret Ship* (Doubleday, 1978), 136
pp.,a high-interest, low-reading-
level book for teenagers, and Peggy
Mann, *Last Road to Safety: A True
Story* (Macmillan, 1975), 32 pp.
(elementary level).

Kohn, Moshe, editor
Jewish Resistance During
the Holocaust:
Proceedings of the Conference
on Manifestations of Jewish
Resistance
Jerusalem: Yad Vashem, 1971,
562 pp.

Over thirty papers and debates
dealing with four main subject
headings: the Jewish struggle till
the beginning of the extermination;
the stand of the Jewish masses (the
general public, political parties, the
youth movements); resistance and
armed struggle (revolts, partisan
activities, Jews in various regular
armed services); rescue attempts.
SC

Kohn, Nahum and Howard Roiter
A Voice From the Forest:
Memoirs of a Jewish Partisan
New York: Holocaust Library, 1980,
288 pp. Also paper. (ADL, also
paper)

The path of a small-town
watchmaker from a religious family
in western Poland to the forest of
Volhynia where, after many narrow
adventures and narrow escapes, he
joins the detachment of the Soviet
partisan Medvedev. JSC

Kulski, Julian Eugeniusz
Dying, We Live:
The Personal Chronicle of
a Young Freedom Fighter
in Warsaw (1939-1945)
New York: Holt, Rinehart & Winston,
1979, 304 pp.

The author, a Christian, was the
ten-year-old son of Warsaw's mayor
when the war began. He joined the
resistance, witnessed the Ghetto
uprising in1943, was jailed by the
Gestapo, fought with the Polish
home army and was a prisoner of
war before he was sixteen. The
book is based on a diary he kept
during the war and memoirs written
immediately after. Includes maps
and photos of the city and of the
Ghetto. JSC

Krakowski, Shmuel
The War of the Doomed: Jewish Armed Resistance in Poland, 1942-1944
New York: Holmes & Meier, 1984, 340 pp.

Emphasizes the uniqueness of this partisan movement which had little or no support from political organizations or anti-Nazi governments, and whose members were often the victims of other partisan groups. Includes a chapter on the participation of Jews in the Warsaw uprising of the summer of 1944. Good concluding summary. C

Lester, Elenore
Wallenberg: the Man in the Iron Web
Englewood Cliffs: Prentice-Hall, 1982, 183 pp. Also paper. (ADL paper)

A carefully researched and well-written "biography-thriller" of the Swedish diplomat. (See Anger, *With Raoul Wallenberg. . .* above.) JSC

Levi, Primo
If Not Now, When
New York: Summit Books, 1985, 346 pp. Cloth.

Levi, the Italian Jewish author of *Survival in Auschwitz,* has written a multifaceted novel based on fact. It is a sad, thrilling, insightful story about a group of East European Jewish partisans who fought back against the Nazis and their collaborators. What the reader can expect from this moving novel is exemplified by the following passage: "The old and sick die, but young and healthy people also die, of despair. Despair is worse than disease; it attacks you during the days of waiting, when no news comes and no contacts, or when they announce German troop movements or movements of Ukrainians: waiting is as fatal as dysentery. There are only two defenses against despair: working and fighting; but they are not always enough." SC

Meed, Vladka
On Both Sides of the Wall
New York: Holocaust Library, 1979, 304 pp. Also paper. (ADL, also paper)

Seventeen-year-old Fegele "Vladka" worked on the "Aryan" side of the underground movement in Nazi-occupied Warsaw. An intelligent and courageous courier, she helped Jews escape from the ghetto, found them shelter in the homes of Christians, established contact with survivors in the woods. SC

Perl, William R.
The Four-Front War:
From the Holocaust to
the Promised Land
New York: Crown, 1979,
376 pp. Also Paper.

Between 1937 and 1945, 40,000 Jews fled from the Holocaust and came to Palestine — illegally. This is the story of the rescue operation, its heroes and villains, underground warfare, intelligence and counter-intelligence by major powers and Betar-Irgun, the Jewish activist organization. The "four fronts" refer to the Nazis, the British, the Jewish establishment and the elements. Told by the man who was the "Action's" chief organizer. JSC

Ramati, Alexander
The Assisi Underground:
The Priests Who Rescued Jews
New York: Stein and Day, 1978,
181 pp.

A peasant turned priest, Father Rufino Niccacci sheltered and protected 300 Jews in the beautiful Italian town of Assisi during the Nazi occupation. The city was saved from destruction by a letter forged by one of the Jewish refugees in which the Wehrmacht declared Assisi an open city. Alexander Ramati, one of the first war correspondents to enter Assisi after the Germans were driven out, relates the story of Fr. Rufino, recipient of

the title of "Righteous Gentile," the highest honor the State of Israel can bestow on a Christian, with enormous sympathy and a sense of drama. JSC

✓*Rose, Leesha*
The Tulips Are Red
New York: Barnes, 1978,
275 pp.

A Dutch Jewish girl just graduated from high school looks forward to a career in medicine, marriage and children. Narrowly escaping deportation, she joins the Dutch resistance. Ms. Rose is a lecturer and guide at Yad Vashem in Jerusalem. JS

✓*Sachs, Marilyn*
A Pocket Full of Seeds
New York: Doubleday, 1973, 144 pp.

A young girl is separated from her parents during the Nazi invasion of France. She is hidden by her headmistress who may be a Nazi sympathizer. Based on a true story. For younger readers. EJ

✓*Samuels, Gertrude*
Mottele: A Partisan Odyssey
New York: Signet/New American Library, 1977, 179 pp. Paper.

Documentary novel based on the lives and deeds of Jewish partisans who fought in the forests of Poland and the Soviet Union in World War II. Revolves around twelve-year-old

Mottele, whose family was destroyed and who joins the Jewish resistance fighters. Miss Samuels, a writer and a consultant to UNICEF in the 1940s, covered the Displaced Persons camps of Europe and met the Holocaust survivors immediately after their release. JS

Senesh, Hannah
Hannah Senesh, Her Life and Diary
Translated from the Hebrew by Marta Cohn. New York: Schocken, 1973, 268 pp.

In 1944, Hungarian-born Hannah Senesh and 31 other Palestinian Jews were parachuted into Nazi-occupied Balkan countries to secure information for the British and to save Jews from the Holocaust. Seven of the 32 were captured and killed; one of them was Hannah Senesh, age 23. This volume includes some of her poetry. (See *Interrogation in Budapest* in A-V section below). JSC

✓*Stadtler, Bea*
The Holocaust: A History of Courage and Resistance
New York. ADL/Behrman House, 1974. Also paper, 210 pp.

Twenty-two simply written chapters about the main events of the Holocaust and the resistance and rescue. Translations of original documents and diaries bring the student into direct relationship with the real people who endured the Holocaust. (Separate discussion guide by N. Karkowsky available from Behrman.) EJS

✓*Suhl, Yuri*
On the Other Side of the Gate
New York: Franklin Watts, 1975, 149 pp. Avon, 1976, 176 pp. Paper.

For a Jew in the ghetto to give birth was against Nazi decrees. Giving birth then became an act of resistance. Smuggling the infant out of the ghetto by the Polish underground gives this novel an extra measure of suspense. JS

✓*Suhl, Yuri, editor and translator*
They Fought Back: The Story of the Jewish Resistance in Nazi Europe
New York: Schocken Books, 1975. 327 pp. Paper. (ADL)

Thirty-three dramatic stories and documents. Tells of organizers and heroes of the Jewish underground, the ghettos, the camps, the partisans. True tales of revolts and escapes. JS

✓*Suhl, Yuri*
Uncle Misha's Partisans
New York: Four Winds Press (Scholastic), 1973, 211 pp.

Twelve-year-old Motele escapes to the woods to join the famous band of Jews known as Uncle Misha's partisans. Based on the lives of a real group of Jewish resistance fighters in the Ukraine, the novel is fast moving, suspenseful. EJS

tenBoom, Corrie with John and Elizabeth Sherrill
The Hiding Place
Boston: G.K. Hall, 1973; Old Tappan, N.J.: Revell, 1974, Bantam, 1974, 256 pp. Paper.

The tenBooms, a deeply religious Christian family, joined the Dutch underground. Their home became a hiding place for Jews. Corrie and her sister were sent to Ravensbruck, a concentration camp for women. JS

Wuorio, Eva-Lis
To Fight in Silence
New York: Holt, Rinehart & Winston, 1973, 216 pp.

Novel about Christian families who opposed the Nazis in Denmark and Norway. EJS

Zassenhaus, Hiltgunt
Walls: Resisting the Third Reich — One Woman's Story
Boston: Beacon Press, 1974, 256 pp. Also paper.

Many Germans were avid Nazis. Most complied either willingly or to "avoid trouble." A few resisted. A graduate in Scandinavian languages, the author was assigned to work censoring the mail of political prisoners from these countries and monitoring prison visits by a Norwegian minister. She recounts how she gradually became involved in aiding them and in resisting the Nazis. JSC

Zucker, Simon, compiler.
Translated and edited by Gertrude Hirshler
The Unconquerable Spirit: Vignettes of the Jewish Religious Spirit the Nazis Could Not Destroy
New York: Zachor Institute, distributed by Mesorah Publications, 1980, 160 pp. Paper.

Incidents in the lives of rabbis, Hasidic rebbes, and "ordinary Orthodox Jews" who defied the Nazis by continuing to teach, to study, to pray and to be concerned with observance of Jewish life, often with the Nazi guns pointed at them. Includes an epilogue and lamentation on the Holocaust in Hebrew and English. JS

AUDIO-VISUAL

Act of Faith
28 minutes/black-and-white/
not cleared for TV/ADL

The dramatic story of the heroic Danish resistance movement against Hitler, originally presented on CBS-TV. Filmed in Denmark, it is a firsthand account of how the Danes saved their Jewish coun-trymen from Nazi extermination. JS

As If It Were Yesterday
85 minutes/black-and-white/
Cinema Five

Thanks to an underground network of courageous Belgian citizens, 4000 Jewish children were spared deportation and extermination dur-ing the Nazi occupation. The film retraces this event and includes interviews with some of the children, now grown men and women, who owe their lives to their heroic countrymen. The film was made by two women whose parents spent the war in hiding. JSC

Avenue of the Just
55 minutes/color/cleared for TV/
ADL

Moving documentary of ten Chris-tians who saved Jewish lives. Some of the rescued recount their per-sonal experiences. Explores the motivations of the rescuers, whose deeds imperiled their friends, families and themselves. Includes individuals originally from Germany, Poland, Belgium, France, Holland. JSC

The Bookseller
30 minutes/kinescope/black-and-white/National Academy

Dramatization of an actual incident based on the book by Harold Flender, *Rescue in Denmark* (see above). Relations between a bookseller-resistance leader and a Gestapo captain who loves the for-bidden Heine. JS

Conspiracy of Hearts
113 minutes/black-and-white/
feature film/Jewish Media Service/
JWB

A group of nuns in a convent in Northern Italy in 1943 help Jewish children escape from a local deten-tion camp. Warm, simple. While not a "true" story, it does reflect the fact that many convents sheltered Jewish youngsters during the war. EJS

Interrogation in Budapest
60 minutes/color/National Academy
Dramatization of life and death of

Hannah Senesh. See the book,
Hannah Senesh, Her Life and Diary
(above). S

Resistance: Jewish Ghetto Fighters and Partisans
18 minutes/filmstrip with cassette
and discussion guide/Jewish
Education Press

A factual overview of the incidents
of armed resistance by the Jewish
ghetto fighters and partisans during
the Holocaust. JS

Watch on the Rhine
114 minutes/black-and-white/JWB
Lecture Bureau

An anti-Nazi underground leader
comes to the United States with his
American wife and children and
finds himself blackmailed. Based
on the play by Lillian Hellman and
starring Bette Davis. SC

War Criminals

The following acts, or any of them, are crimes coming within the jurisdiction of the Tribunal for which there shall be individual responsibility . . . (c) CRIMES AGAINST HUMANITY: namely, murder, extermination, enslavement, deportation, and other inhumane acts committed against any civilian population, before or during the war; or persecutions on political, racial or religious grounds in execution of or in connection with any crime within the jurisdiction of the Tribunal, whether or not in violation of the domestic law of the country where perpetrated.

Leaders, organizers, instigators and accomplices participating in the formulation or execution of a common plan or conspiracy to commit any of the foregoing crimes are responsible for all acts performed by any persons in execution of such plan.

The Nuremberg Tribunal

PUBLICATIONS

Blum, Howard
Wanted! The Search for Nazis in America
New York: Crest/Fawcett, 1978. Paper; Times Books, 1977, 256 pp. Paper.

True story of four Nazis who came to this country after the war, the life they led here and the men who tracked them down. Tells of stolen government records, immigration and court delays, State Department inaction. Focuses on the pivotal figure of Anthony DeVito, Immigration Service investigator who helped bring these criminals to justice. JSC

Borkin, Joseph
**The Crime and
Punishment of
I.G. Farben**
New York: The Free Press, 1978,
332 pp.

The giant cartel of I.G. Farben
developed nerve gas, introduced
slave labor at Auschwitz, developed
synthetic fuel and gun powder for
the Third Reich, and plundered the
chemical industries of conquered
countries. Its successor company is
larger now than Farben was in its
heyday. "Forces one to consider the
possibility that when corporate evil
reaches a certain status, it simply
cannot be defeated." (New York
Times) JSC

Ferencz, Benjamin B.
**Less than Slaves:
Jewish Forced
Labor and the Quest for
Compensation**
Cambridge, MA: Harvard University
Press, 1979, 249 pp. Also Paper,
1982, 280 pp.

An American prosecutor at the
Nuremberg trials writes of the com-
plicity between the SS and major
German industrial firms in the prof-
itable exploitation of concentration
camp labor and the unwillingness
of these companies to acknowledge
either legal
or moral responsibility.
SC

Gilbert, G.M.
Nuremberg Diary
New York: Farrar, Straus & Giroux,
1947; Signet, 1971, 430 pp. New
American Library. Paper.

An account of the first Nuremberg
trials plus interviews with the
prisoners. The author was a psychologist of the International
Military Tribunal and spent long
hours in conversation with the
major war criminals. JSC

Harel, Isser
The House on Garibaldi Street
New York: Viking, 1975, 296 pp.;
Bantam, 1976. Paper.

The true account of the 15-year
quest to capture Adolf Eichmann, in
hiding in Argentina, and bring him
to trial in Israel. The author is former head of the Israeli Secret Service. Reads like a fiction thriller. JS

Hausner, Gideon
Justice in Jerusalem
New York: Herzl, 1978; Holocaust
Library, 1978, 560 pp. Paper. (ADL,
Paper)

The trial of Adolf Eichmann, key
official in the Nazi hierarchy, upon
whom his superiors had imposed
the principal responsibility for carrying out the "Final Solution of the
Jewish question." Told against the
background of the history of the
Holocaust by the man who was
then Attorney General of Israel and
the prosecuting attorney at the trial.
SC

Klarsfeld, Beate
Wherever They May Be!
New York: Vanguard Press, 1975,
344 pp.

A German Christian born on the eve
of World War II, married to a French
Jew who witnessed the Nazi terror
and whose father was gassed at
Auschwitz, Beate Klarsfeld has conducted her own crusade against
Nazi criminals still at large. Her
book chronicles the passionate and
relentless search for these butchers
that has earned her Israel's Medal
of Courage and stands as proof
that the voice of one person of
moral conviction can be heard. SC

Knoop, Hans
The Menten Affair
New York: Macmillan, 1978, 164
pp.

The author, a Dutch journalist,
tracks down and helps bring Pieter
Menten, a multimillionaire art
collector, to trial for taking part in
the Nazi killing of Polish Jews during World War II. Menten was con-
victed. JSC

Noble, Iris
Nazi Hunter: Simon Wiesenthal
New York: Julius Messner, 1979,
159 pp.

Since the end of World War II,
Simon Wiesenthal has dedicated
his life to tracking down Nazi war
criminals. This book, which reads
like an espionage story, tells the

story of several of Wiesenthal's suc-
cesses — including identifying the
Gestapo officer who arrested Anne
Frank and her family. EJS

Ruffini, Gene
The Choice
New York: ADL, 1980, 83 pp.
Typescript.

A two-act play set in a teenage
runaway shelter in Greenwich
Village run by a former SS killer-
turned-priest. Using "role-playing"
as therapy, the runaways re-enact
their pasts — neglect, abuse, pros-
titution. A survivor comes to bring
the priest to justice. What is justice
in this case? Powerful. Language
abusive. Good vehicle for group discussion. C

Sereny, Gitta
**Into That Darkness: An
Examination of Conscience**
New York: Vintage, 1983, 400 pp.
Paper.

A portrait of the life of Franz Stangl,
Commandant of Sobibor and
Treblinka concentration camps —
the only Nazi Commandant ever to
come to trial. Based on 70 hours of
interviews with Stangl and extensive follow-up research. SC

Wiesenthal, Simon
**The Sunflower: With a
Symposium**
New York: Schocken, 1977, 216 pp.
Also paper.

Allegory by the famous hunter of

Nazi war criminals which poses painful questions. A young Jew is taken from a death camp to a makeshift army hospital and placed next to a dying Nazi who extends his hand toward the Jew. The novel forms the basis for a symposium which is part two of the volume. Participants in the symposium were asked to express an opinion on the moral issue posed in the story. Participants include Abraham J. Heschel, Martin E. Marty, Cynthia Ozick, Herbert Marcuse, Msgr. John M. Oesterreicher. JSC

Wiesenthal, Simon
The Murderers Among Us:
The Wiesenthal Memoirs
New York: McGraw-Hill, 1967, 340 pp.; Bantam, 1973. Paper.

Wiesenthal is the organizer of a documentation center whose major aim is searching for missing German war criminals. Includes his fascinating pursuit of Adolf Eichmann. Edited, with a substantial profile of the subject, by Joseph Wechsberg. JSC

AUDIO-VISUAL

The Demjanjuk Trial: A Moment in History
15 minutes/color/video cassette/ discussion guide

In 1981, John Demjanjuk was brought to trial in Cleveland, Ohio, accused of concealing his Nazi past when he came to the United States more than a quarter of a century ago. In a documentary produced by the *Cleveland Jewish News,* the evidence against Demjanjuk is presented, testimony by the survivors of the Treblika death camp is heard, and the effects of the trial on Cleveland's Jewish and Ukrainian communities are analyzed. Accompanied by a detailed study guide, this production is an effective discussion stimulator—for classroom and adult group use—on the question of

continued pursuit of Nazi war criminals, now that more than forty years have passed. In February 1986, Demjanjuk was extridated to stand trial in Israel. JSC

Judgment at Mineola
14 minutes/color/ADL

Boleslav Maikovskis, an accused Nazi war criminal, has lived in Mineola, Long Island, since he came to this country from Latvia in 1951. In 1971, immigration authorities began deportation hearings. Mike Wallace and a CBS "60 Minutes" crew confronted some Mineola residents with a record of the atrocities Maikovskis committed. The opinions they expressed include: "He's suffered long enough with this inside himself." "If a person commits a crime he must pay for it." "Why don't you just forget it?" Discussion stimulator. JSC

Judgment at Nuremberg
186 minutes/16mm/
black-and-white/feature film/
United Artists

Fictionalized account of the trial of Nazi war criminals which serves as a case study of Germany during the Holocaust. Provides insight into the issues of freedom of choice, obedience to authority, and responsibility to mankind. JSC

Judgment at Nuremberg—Filmstrip
3 parts/160 frames each/
20 minutes each/cassettes/ADL

From the film (see above). Includes Study Guide. JS

The Last Nazi
71 minutes/color and
black-and-white/
Learning Corporation of America

Several years after his release from Spandau Prison, where he completed a 20-year sentence for war crimes, Albert Speer is interviewed by Canadian reporter Patrick Watson. Chronicles through newsreel footage the rise and fall of the Nazi regime and Speer's mentality and career; also sheds light on the behavior of many Germans who fell under Hitler's spell. Intelligent, sophisticated, now reflective, Speer presents a rational account of how it happened. The film investigates issues relating to loyalty, power, obedience to authority, ambition, etc. The viewers must decide as historians using the tools of critical thinking how they will accept explanations offered by Albert Speer. SC

The Nuremberg War Crimes Trial
15 photographs/Social Studies
School Service

Presents scenes surrounding the trial of the more notorious German leaders, including the courtroom, prison, security personnel, prosecutors and prisoners. Printed on 11" x 14" heavy glossy stock. Captions. JS

Verdict for Tomorrow
28 minutes/black-and-white/ADL

A well-documented account of the Eichmann trial, narrated by Lowell Thomas. The film is based on the actual footage gathered during the Eichmann trial in Jerusalem. It utilizes the trial as a reminder of Nazism and Jewish persecution rather than as a "dated" legal presentation. Produced by Capitol Cities Broadcasting Company. JSC

War Crimes
Filmstrip/cassette/teacher's guide/
Zenger Productions

Attempts to help students understand the nature of international law. Through the study and comparison of the war crimes and trials of German and Japanese leaders after World War II, and crimes in Vietnam, including the trial of Lt. Calley, students learn that there are no simple answers to questions of morality. JS

War Crimes
15 11 x 14 photo aids/
1 color filmstrip/record or
cassettes and teacher's guide/
Documentary Photo Aids.

Also available, photo aids alone.
JS

Survivors and the Generation After

*true, we are the children
of a nocturnal twilight
the heirs of Auschwitz and Ponar
but ours is also the rainbow:
in us the storm meets sunlight
to create new colors
as we add defiant sparks
to an eternal fire*

**Menachem Z. Rosensaft
Child of survivors**

PUBLICATIONS

Bauer, Yehuda
**Flight and Rescue: Brichah
The Organized Escape of
the Jewish Survivors of
Eastern Europe, 1944-1948**
New York: Random House, 1970,
369 pp. (ADL)

Fully documented, detailed history of the mass movement of almost 300,000 Jewish survivors by a clandestine underground organization. In their search for survival the exiles often clashed with postwar occupying powers. Many thousands reached Palestine. SC

Bergmann, Martin and Milton E. Jucovy
Generations of the Holocaust
New York: Basic Books, 1982,
338 pp.

The major portion of this highly specialized book has been distilled from the work of the Group for the Psychoanalytic Study of the Effect of the Holocaust on the Second Generation. The purpose of the group is to pursue an ongoing, in-depth investigation of how the trauma inflicted on victims of the Holocaust could be transmitted from one generation to another. Included are studies of children of Nazi perpetrators. Includes anecdotal material which helps make this difficult book more accessible to the layperson. C

Brenner, Robert Reeve
**The Faith and Doubt of
Holocaust Survivors**
New York: The Free Press, 1980,
266 pp.

A study based on questionnaires and interviews with camp and ghetto survivors that deals only with survivors living in Israel. But because Jews living in Israel have been through several wars in the past four decades, their situation is very special. It cannot be assumed therefore that this book describes the faith and doubts of survivors living elsewhere. The statistical information is not that helpful, but the excerpts from interviews are strong enough to sustain one's interest and provide insights into the lives of these survivors. C

Chaneles, Sol
Three Children of the Holocaust
New York: Avon, 1974,
192 pp. Paper.

A novel of two girls and a boy, orphaned survivors of the Holocaust who have almost no remembrance of their life before the camps. The three are adopted by a wealthy American Jewish couple. It is primarily the story of their life after the Holocaust, and of not remembering. Strange and, at times, disturbing. SC

Eliach, Yaffa, and Uri Assaf
The Last Jew
New York: Smadar, 1977; Israel: Alef-Alef Multi Media Production, 1977, 138 pp. Paper.

A play which depicts the different ways two generations (those who were "there" and the next genera- tion of children) react to the trauma of the Nazi Holocaust. SC

Epstein, Helen
Children of the Holocaust: Conversations with Sons and Daughters of the Survivors
New York: G.P. Putnam's Sons, 1979, 348 pp.; Bantam, 1980, 348 pp. Paper.

Within the last decade, more than a score of children of survivor groups have sprung up all over the country. They are just beginning to identify themselves. The author is herself a child of sur- vivors. JCS

Hannam, Charles
A Boy in that Situation: An Autobiography
New York: Harper & Row, 1978, 217 pp.

An unsentimental account of a Jewish boy growing up in Germany in the 30's. He fled Germany in 1939 and is today a professor of education in Great Britain. JS

Kanfer, Stefan
The Eighth Sin
New York: Random House, 1978, 288 pp.; Berkley, 277 pp. Paper.

A novel about a Gypsy boy who sur- vived the camps. Adopted by a Jewish couple, he comes to New York and plans revenge against the man who once saved him. Absorbing. JSC

Kerr, Judith
When Hitler Stole Pink Rabbit
New York: Coward, McCann and
Geoghegan, 1972, Putnam.

A novel based on the author's
experience. She was born in Berlin,
where her father was a drama critic.
The family left Germany in 1933
when Anna was 9 years old,
arriving in England in 1936.
For younger readers. E

Kerr, Judith
The Other Way Round
New York: Coward, McCann and
Geoghegan, 1975, 256 pp.; Dell,
1979, 240 pp.
Paper.

Continues the story of *When Hitler
Stole Pink Rabbit.* Anna, now an
adult, returns to Berlin at the height
of the Hungarian and Suez crises
in 1956. She finds herself trying to
deal with questions of life and
death and rediscovers the past in
the world of those who survived the
Holocaust. EJ

Klepfisz, Irena
Keeper of Accounts
Watertown, MA:
Sinister Wisdom Books,
1982, 98 pp. Paper.

A major section of this volume of
poetry relates to the Holocaust.
These are beautiful, moving, evoca-
tive works. The author was born in
the Warsaw Ghetto in 1941.
JSC

Leitner, Isabella
**Saving the Fragments: From
Auschwitz to New York**
New York: New American Library,
1985, 131 pp. Cloth.

A sequel to *Fragments of Isabella.*
With immediacy and passion the
author recreates her journey from
liberation by the Red Army to the
reunion with her father and the
beginning of a new life. JSC

Murray, Michele
The Crystal Nights
New York: Clarion/Houghton-Mifflin,
1973, 320 pp.

A German-Jewish family escapes
from Germany and comes to an
American farm to live with relatives,
some of whom are Christian. Novel
explores teenage relationships. EJS

Pincus, Chasya
**Come From the Four Winds:
The Story of Youth Aliya**
New York: Herzl Press, 1970,
333 pp.

In 1933, the growth of Nazi anti-
Semitism and the increasing restric-
tions imposed on Jews gave rise
to an organization whose goal
was to bring teenage youngsters
from Hitler's Germany to the
kibbutzim (collective set-
tlements) in Palestine. Since its
inception, Youth Aliya has brought
more than 120,000 youngsters to
Israel — including, since the
1950's, many from the Middle East.

This book tells the dramatic story of Youth Aliya and of some of the people whose lives were saved. EJS

Pisar, Samuel
Of Blood and Hope
Boston: Little, Brown, 1980, 311 pp.

When the war ended, Pisar was a 16-year-old survivor of Auschwitz. Today, he is an international lawyer who has participated in high-level U.S. and intergovernmental conferences. His Holocaust experiences forced him to find the physical and intellectual resources within himself to survive and succeed. The first section of the book recounts the Holocaust years. The rest is about his life after the war. Throughout, the author shares his geopolitical philosophy, his fears and his hopes. SC

Rabinowitz, Dorothy
New Lives: Survivors of the Holocaust Living in America
New York: Alfred A. Knopf, 1976, 242 pp.; Avon, 1976, 240 pp. Paper.

A well-written and fascinating book containing the personal stories of Holocaust survivors living in America. Provides important insights into the dilemmas faced by the victims, and the lasting effects of their experiences. Includes material on the Eichmann trial and the 1972 deportation hearings of

Hermine Braunsteiner Ryan, the Queens, N.Y. housewife who was deputy commander at two concentration camps. Not difficult reading, but may be conceptually difficult for some. JSC

Reiss, Johanna
The Journey Back
New York: Harper & Row, 1976, 214 pp.

Sequel to *The Upstairs Room* (see section on Camps, Ghettos, In Hiding, above). The first year of peace and the resiliency of the human spirit. EJ

Rothschild, Sylvia, editor
Voices From the Holocaust
Foreword by Elie Wiesel.
New York: New American Library, 1981, 456 pp.

Several institutions have projects recording oral testimony from survivors (and liberators). This volume was culled from over 650 hours of tapes (2500 pages of transcription) recorded by survivors in various parts of this country under the auspices of the William E. Wiener Oral History Library of the American Jewish Committee. The book is divided into three parts—life before the Holocaust, life during the Holocaust and life in America. Especially interesting are how these "refugees" see themselves as Jews and as Americans, and how they view the American Jewish community. The book invites comparison (the contributors are from diverse backgrounds and experiences) and reflection. JSC

Segal, Lore
Other People's Houses
New York: Harcourt Brace, 1964, 312 pp.; New American Library, 1973. Paper.

Nine months after Hitler entered Austria, a ten-year-old Jewish girl, with a cardboard label marked 152 strung on a shoelace around her neck, boarded a train in Vienna that was to take several hundred children westward to safety. Lore reached England, and for seven years lived in "other people's houses." Meanwhile, her parents managed to escape and they, too, lived in England in "other people's houses" as servants. In 1948 they went to live in the Dominican Republic — and in the 1950's their quota numbers for immigration to the U.S. came through. JS

Singer, Isaac Bashevis
Enemies, A Love Story
New York: Farrar, Straus & Giroux, 1972, 288 pp. Also paper; Crest/Fawcett, 1977.

The traumatic effects of the Holocaust pursue the protagonists of this forceful novel as they attempt to make a new life for themselves in the United States after the war. The complex personality of the hero and his entanglements with his three wives are woven together with powerful evocations of Jewish life in Poland and in New York City by the Nobel Prize-winning author in his usually compelling style. For very mature students only. C

Steinitz, Lucy Y. and David M. Szonyi, editors
Living After the Holocaust: Reflections by the Post-War Generation
New York: Bloch, 1976, 149 pp. Also paper.

In essays, poetry, and interviews, children of survivors write about the Holocaust, their parents, themselves and the special responsibility they feel to "bring joy" to their parents. JSC

Styron, William
Sophie's Choice
New York: Random House, 1980, 515 pp.; Bantam, 1982, 640 pp. Paper.

A major American novelist intertwines the stories of Sophie, a Polish Catholic survivor of the camps; Nathan, a brilliant, mad Jewish scientist; and the author, a young man from the South growing up, after the war, in New York. Through the experiences of Sophie, a non-Jew, Styron seeks to portray the Holocaust as a universal phenomenon. For mature readers. SC

Traub, Barbara Fischman
The Matrushka Doll
New York: Richard Marek, 1979,
487 pp.

Absorbing novel that begins with
the liberation of the camps and
ends one year later, in May 1946,
When the Iron Curtain descends
over Eastern Europe. The focus is
on coming home (in this case to the
town of Sighet in Transylvania) and
on the reception the Jewish
survivors received. SC

Uris, Leon
Exodus
New York: Doubleday, 1958; Ban-
tam, 1981, 608 pp. Paper.

An epic novel concerning the smuggling of camp survivors into Palestine before it became Israel.
Shifting scenes from detention
camps at Cyprus, to a Palestine
kibbutz, to underground Mossad
Aliyah which purchased boats, to
memories of survivors. An engrossing story. JSC

Wiesel, Elie
The Fifth Son
New York: Summit Books, 1985,
220 pp. Cloth.

This is a searing tale of an
American Jew struggling to understand his father-survivor's torment.
The father's anguish springs from
the memory of participating in the
murder of an SS officer in order to
avenge a death. When the son dis-
covers that the SS officer is still
alive in Germany, he travels there to
confront his father's nightmarish
past. Winner of the Paris Grand
Prize for Literature. JSC

AUDIO-VISUAL

Exodus
207 minutes/color/feature film/
United Artists/JWB Lecture Bureau

Based on the Uris book (see above)
starring Paul Newman, Eva Marie
Saint, Sal Mineo. Directed by Otto
Preminger. JSC

In Dark Places:
Remembering the Holocaust
58 minutes/color/Phoenix Films

Explores the attempts of a few
individuals to come to terms with
the Holocaust. Among them are the
survivors of the ghettos and concentration camps and their children;
members of the New Artef Players
performing and discussing their
play based on the experiences of
the survivors; and writer and social
critic, Susan Sontag, who places the
event in a social and historical context, showing how the imagery of
the Holocaust has become part of
our cultural baggage — in movies,
art, political rhetoric, popular fads

and fashion. Gina Blumenfeld, the producer and director, is a child of survivors. SC

The Pawnbroker
114 minutes/black-and-white/
feature film/ Audio Brandon/
JWB Lecture Bureau

This film offers a portrait of a man who survived a Nazi concentration camp, only to encounter further horrors in New York City. Rod Steiger won an Oscar nomination for his performance as Sol Nazerman — a Jewish pawnbroker who has lost faith in God and his fellow man. A social worker and Nazerman's young assistant try to penetrate the wall of bitterness Nazerman has built around himself. Until an unforgettably dramatic moment in which the old man suddenly realizes his responsibility to humanity.

After the Holocaust: Reflections and Literary Analyses

That which has happened is a warning. To forget it is guilt. It must be continually remembered. It was possible for this to happen, and it remains possible for it to happen again at any minute. Only in knowledge can it be prevented.

**Karl Jaspers
20th Century German
philosopher**

PUBLICATIONS

Amery, Jean
**At the Mind's Limits:
Contemplations by a Survivor
on Auschwitz and its Realities**
Translated from the German
by Sidney Rosenfeld and Stella P.
Rosenfeld.
Bloomington, Indiana: Indiana
University Press, 1980, 128 pp.
(ADL) Paper, Schocken

Five compelling, painful, thought-provoking essays by an assimilated intellectual Viennese Jew: At the Mind's Limits; Torture; How much Home does a Person Need; Resentments; On the Necessity and Impossibility of Being a Jew.
SC

Berkovits, Eliezer
Faith After the Holocaust
New York: KTAV, 1973, 180 pp.
(ADL, Paper)

This book speaks to the question of retaining one's religious belief after the horrors of the Holocaust. In the author's words "We are not Job and we dare not speak and respond as if we were. We are only Job's brother. We must believe because our brother Job believed; and we must question, because our brother Job so often could not believe any longer. This is not a comfortable situation; but it is our condition in this era after the Holocaust."
SC

Bosmajian, Hamida
Metaphors of Evil:
Contemporary German
Literature
and the Shadow of Nazism
Iowa City: University of Iowa Press,
1979, 247 pp. Also paper.

Highly sophisticated analysis of the
intellectual and emotional defenses
of contemporary German culture as
revealed in the form and content of
literary structure in the wake of the
Holocaust. An attempt to determine
the impact of the Nazi era on the
literary imagination. Teacher. C

Cargas, James, editor
Responses to Elie Wiesel
New York: Persea, 1978,
286 pp. Also paper.
(ADL, also paper.)

Sixteen Jewish and Christian writers
and scholars discuss Wiesel's
works. Contributors include Robert
McAfee Brown, Maurice Friedman,
Thomas A. Idinopulos, Lawrence L.
Langer. SC

Cohen, Arthur A.
Arguments and Doctrines:
A Reader in Jewish Thinking
After The Holocaust
New York: Harper and Row, 1970,
541 pp.

Twenty-eight essays on the search
for meaning in Judaism, Jewish
life and the Jewish people by an
imposing array of Jewish historians,
political scientists, critics,
philosophers, atheists and rabbis.
Among the contributors: J.L.
Talmon, Will Herberg, Hannah
Arendt, Hans Schoeps, Gershom
Scholem. The editor's comments
add to the intellectual and
philosophical challenge of this
collection. C

DeKoven Ezrahi, Sidra
By Words Alone: The Holocaust
in Literature
Chicago: University of Chicago,
1980, 275 pp. Cloth and Paper.
Foreword by Alfred Kazin

In this highly acclaimed study, the
author examines a wide range of
literature — novels, poetry, short
stories, and plays — written in
English, Yiddish, Hebrew, German,
French, etc. While essentially a
literary history, *By Words Alone* is
also a reflective work. C

Fackenheim, Emil L.
God's Presence in History:
Jewish Affirmation and
Philosophical Reflections
New York: Torch/Harper & Row,
1972, 104 pp. Paper.

"The trauma of contemporary
events affects all religious belief. It
is Jewish religious belief, however,
which is most traumatically affected. Jews were murdered, not
because they had disobeyed the
God of history, but rather because
their great-grandparents had

obeyed Him. Dare a Jew of today continue to obey the God of history — and thus expose to the danger of a second Auschwitz himself, his children and his children's children?" C

Fackenheim, Emil L.
The Jewish Return into History: Reflections in the Age of Auschwitz and a New Jerusalem
New York: Schocken, 1980, 312 pp. Paper.

This collection of essays deals with the implications of the Holocaust for Jewish faith and life, and the ethical challenge and touchstone it represents for both Jews and non-Jews. From the horrors of the Holocaust to the founding of modern Israel, the author shows the deep connection, in history and in faith, between these two events. C

Fleischner, Eva, editor
Auschwitz: Beginning of a New Era?
Reflections of the Holocaust
New York: KTAV, Cathedral and ADL, 1977, 469 pp. Paper.

Originally presented at the International Symposium on the Holocaust held at the Cathedral of St. John the Divine in New York City. Major papers on Theological Reflections on the Holocaust; the History of Christian Theology and the Demonization of the Jews;

Christian Mission in Crisis; Judaism and Christian Education; Theological Reflections on the State of Israel in the Light of the Yom Kippur War; Radical Theology, the New Left and Israel; The New Romanticism and Biblical Faith; Auschwitz and the Pathology of Jew-Hatred; Blacks and Jews; Affinity and Confrontation; Art and Culture after the Holocaust. Contributors include Alfred Kazin, Rosemary Ruether, Gregory Baum, Yosef Yerushalmi, Allan Davis, Irving Greenberg, John Pawlikowski, Shlomo Avineri, Paul Jacobs, Milton Himmelfarb, Michael Ryan, Arthur Waskow, Charles Silberman, Elie Wiesel.
C

Insdorf, Annette
Indelible Shadows: Film and the Holocaust
New York: Random House, 1983, 234 pp. Paper.

Richly illustrated with more than 140 movie stills, this book is a useful introduction to the ways in which film makers have dealt with the Holocaust. Explores 75 fictional and documentary films, primarily from the U.S., France, Germany, Italy and Poland. The book intends to explore films rather than to arrive at new historical insights. East European films are not covered as well as they could have been. Good teacher resource. SC

Langer, Lawrence L.
**The Holocaust and the
Literary Imagination**
New Haven: Yale University Press,
1975, 336 pp. Also paper.

"Dachau and Auschwitz as historical phenomena have altered not
only our conception of reality, but
its very nature. The challenge to the
literary imagination is to find a way
of making this fundamental truth
accessible to the mind and
emotions of the reader. The uniqueness of the experience of the
Holocaust may be arguable, but
beyond dispute is the fact that
many writers perceived it as unique,
and began with the premise that
they were working with raw
materials unprecedented in the
literature of history and the history
of literature. The result is a body of
writing that forms the subject of
this study. This book represents a
consciously limited attempt to
impose some critical order on a
selected number of imaginative
works which grew out of that
experience." C

Lasansky, Mauricio
The Nazi Drawings
Iowa City: University of Iowa Press,
1976.

Thirty disturbing, powerful drawings
of death and human deprivation —
Nazi killers, agonized infants, a pros-
titute strung up like a side of beef,
hanged and gassed figures, a
maternal figure impaled by
newsprint cross. Includes an essay by
Edwin Hoenig. When not on tour,
the drawings are housed at the
University of Iowa Museum of Art.
Not for children.
SC

Levi, Primo
The Periodic Table
New York: Schocken Books, 1984,
233 pp. Cloth.

Using the chemical elements of the
periodic table as an allegorical and
guiding motif, the author of *Survival
in Auschwitz* self-consciously recon-
tructs — and thereby finds meaning
in — his Italian Jewish past, his
family, and the events surrounding
his deportation to Auschwitz. It is a
beautifully crafted, original and
imaginatively powerful book.
SC

Pawlikowski, John T.
**The Challenge
of the Holocaust
for Christian Theology**
New York: ADL, 1979,
39 pp. Paper.

Discusses man's responsibility for
"co-creatorship" of the universe
along with God and the potential for
human destructiveness demon-
strated in the death camps, and
implications of the Holocaust for
the status and integrity of the
Church.
C

Rosenfeld, Alvin H.
A Double Dying:
Reflections on Holocaust
Literature
Bloomington and London: Indiana
University Press, 1980,
210 pp. (ADL)

This clearly written study raises and
seeks to answer several fundamental questions about Holocaust
literature: Who are its significant
authors? What are its major
themes? Can we distinguish between its "good" and "bad" books?
Which exploit? Which are authentic?
Which spurious? Can Holocaust
literature be "literary"? Can it afford
not to be? A most useful source for
teachers, librarians and serious
students — even though one may
not always agree with the author's
point of view.
SC

Rosenfeld, Alvin and
Irving Greenberg
Confronting the Holocaust:
The Impact of Elie Wiesel
Bloomington, Ind.: University of
Indiana Press, 1978,
239 pp. (ADL)

This volume seeks to extend and
deepen the exploration of Wiesel's
corpus and the problematics of
Holocaust literature. Among the 14
essayists: Terrence des Pres, Emil
Fackenheim, A. Roy Eckardt, Andre
Neher.
C

Rosenfeld, Alvin
Imagining Hitler
Bloomington: Indiana University
Press, 117 pp. Cloth.

Rosenfeld explores presentations of
Hitler and Nazism in contemporary
high and low culture. He addresses
the questions: What accounts for
the Nazi hold on our imaginations?
Why does Hitler preoccupy us so,
especially in shapes which are
usually fiction? What does Hitler
symbolize today? See also S.
Friedlander's *Reflections on Nazism:*
An Essay on Kitsch and Death.
SC

Roskies, David
Against the Apocalypse
Cambridge: Harvard University
Press, 1984, 374 pp. Cloth.

A formidable challenge to the view
of the Holocaust as an apocalyptic
event, standing outside history,
without analogy or precedent. With
considerable lucidity, Roskies
places the Holocaust, and the
literary responses of victims and
survivors, in the context of
generations of Jewish response to
persecutions, pogroms, and communal catastrophes. A powerful
demonstration showing literature
and culture as a bridge over catastrophe; or, as Roskies puts it, as an
"attempt to make Torah out of history." Awarded the Ralph Waldo
Emerson Prize.
C

Roskies, David
**Night Words: A Midrash
on the Holocaust**
Washington, DC: B'nai B'rith, 1971,
59 pp. Paper.

Poetry in English, Hebrew and Yiddish (with translations), music and midrashic tales from a variety of sources woven into a moving dramatic whole. SC

Rubenstein, Richard L.
After Auschwitz: Radical Theology and Contemporary Judaism
Indianapolis: Bobbs-Merrill, 1966,
289 pp. Paper.

The death camps were a turning point in history that subverted all previous concepts of God and the meaning of human history. Provocative and probing essays. SC

Shur, Irene, G. and
Franklin H. Littell, special editors
Reflections on the Holocaust
Philadelphia: Annals of the American Academy of Political and Social Science, 1980, Holocaust section, 256 pp. complete issue, 315 pp.

Twenty-four scholars from the United States, West Germany, Canada, and Israel contribute to this special issue of *Annals*. They address themselves to questions about the Holocaust, the role of the Churches, attempts of the German nation to rehabilitate itself, implications for public and pro-fessional morality, and how to teach about the Holocaust. SC

Stein, Sol
The Resort
New York: Dell, 1981,
300 pp. Paper.

For "resort" read "concentration camp." Can it happen here? Fiction. SC

Wiesel, Elie
One Generation After
New York: Schocken, 1982,
198 pp. Paper.

Tales, dialogues and memories sparked by the author's return to Sighet, the town of his boyhood, 25 years after he was sent to Auschwitz. JSC

Wiesel, Elie
Against Silence: The Voice and Vision of Elie Wiesel
Selected and edited by Irving Abrahamson
New York: Holocaust Library
Three Volumes, 1219 pp. 1985

Wiesel's essays, lectures, speeches, book reviews, letters, and interviews, not previously published in book form. Subjects include the Holocaust, Jewish identity, Jerusalem, Jewish and world history, youth, Israel, Soviet Jewry, Hasidism, etc. Also includes his addresses and statements as Chairperson of the President's Commission on the Holocaust and the United States Holocaust Memorial Council. A valuable collection. SC

Nature of Human Behavior

Intergroup relations and experiences during World War II have put before us a series of fundamental questions: How far-reaching and penetrating are the teachings of humanity and merciful compassion? Why did not thousands of years of ethical education and concern ward off the horrible massacres or prevent the participation in them of so many "civilized" and "educated" peoples? At what point does the conscience of "normal human beings" compel them to resist evil at the risk of their own lives? In such critical moments how valid and how effective are the feelings of humanity and solidarity among distressed groups?

Philip Friedman
Roads to Extinction

PUBLICATIONS

Bettelheim, Bruno
The Informed Heart: Autonomy in a Mass Age
New York: The Free Press, 1960, 209 pp: Avon, 1971. Paper.

Only the last two chapters are of direct relevance. Based on the author's personal experience in Dachau and Buchenwald in the 1930's. Bettelheim offers an analysis of the psychological factors which subdued many Jews in Europe when the Nazis began their program of mass extermination. Controversial. SC

Bettelheim, Bruno
Surviving and Other Essays
New York: Knopf, 1979. 433 pp.

Includes essays dealing with German concentration camps, the Holocaust one generation later, extreme situations, the ignored lesson of Anne Frank, Eichmann, the system, the victims, surviving, and the psychological appeal of totalitarianism. SC

Cohen, Elie A.
Human Behavior in the Concentration Camp
Translated from the Dutch. Westport, CT: Greenwood, 1984, reprint of 1953 edition; Grosset & Dunlap (Universal Library paperback), 1953, 295 pp.

A valuable study of concentration camp society by a Jewish survivor of Auschwitz and Mauthausen. Originally a thesis in psychiatry at the University of Utrecht, this analysis emphasizes psychological motivations and reactions. C

Des Pres, Terrence
The Survivor: An Anatomy of Life in the Death Camps
New York: Oxford University Press, 1976. Also paper.

Studying eyewitness reports and talking with former inmates, Des Pres suggests that the most significant fact about the struggle for survival is that it depended on fixed activities: on forms of social bonding and interchange, on collective resistance, on keeping dignity and moral sense active. Some have taken issue with his hypothesis. SC

Frankl, Viktor E.
Man's Search for Meaning: An Introduction to Logotherapy
New York: Pocket Books, 1980. Paper.

First-hand account of his experience in Auschwitz. Section on logotherapy heavy going even for above-average seniors. Conceptual level in first part applicable for average 9-12 grade students; second part could be used with above-average juniors and seniors. SC

Fromm, Erich
Escape from Freedom
New York: Avon, 1971. Paper.

According to the author, if a man cannot stand freedom, he will probably turn Fascist. See chapter 6, on "Psychology of Nazism." SC

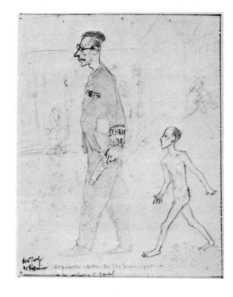

Aldo Carpi, *Little Jewish Boy, Block 31, 1945*

Hoffer, Eric
The True Believer
New York: Harper & Row, 1951,
176 pp. Also paper, 1966.

A classic analysis of the nature of
mass movements and who joins
them. JSC

Kren, George N. and Leon
Rappoport
**The Holocaust and the Crisis of
Human Behavior**
New York: Holmes and Meier,
1980, 200 pp.

Identifies and analyzes psychological and historical factors that led to
the Holocaust. An interdisciplinary
and philosophical perspective are
used in an attempt to provide new insights into the behavior of Holocaust
policy planners and SS personnel.
Analyzes the action of apparently
passive victims, active resisters and
indifferent bystanders, paying special attention to the twin myths of
victim passivity and SS psycho-
pathology. One conclusion: "The
conventional and moral structures
of law and religion have little or no
meaning when set against the
authority of the state." C

Milgram, Stanley
**Obedience to Authority: An
Experimental View**
New York: Harper & Row, 1975,
320 pp. Also paper.

A controversial experiment conducted by the Yale psychologist which
strongly suggests that we are highly
conditioned to do as we are told by
authority figures — even to do
things we know are wrong. C

AUDIO-VISUAL

Hangman
12 minutes/color/McGraw-Hill/
Jewish Media Service-JWB

An allegorical poem in which the
coward in the film, who has let
others die to protect himself,
becomes the Hangman's final victim. Animated film based on
Maurice Ogden's poem. Questions
the individual's moral responsibility in today's world. JS

**An Inquiry Into the Nature of
Man: His Humanity and
Inhumanity**
2 filmstrips/color/cassettes or
records/Center for Humanities

A broad historical survey of man's
complex and beautiful creations as
well as the terrible destruction he
has wrought. Fine use of art and
classical references. S

Man and His Values: An Inquiry into Good and Evil

2 filmstrips/color/cassettes or records/Center for Humanities

An exploration of man's diverse values viewed from one culture to another and from one time period to another, showing how these values originate and change because of contemporary influences. S

Analogies

. . . when the cars began to start and the conductor cried out, "all who are going on this train must get aboard without delay," the colored people cried out with one voice as though the heavens and earth were coming together, and it was so pitiful, that those hardhearted white men who had been accustomed to driving slaves all their lives, shed tears like children. As the cars moved away we heard the weeping and wailing from the slaves, as far as human voice can be heard; and from that time to the present I have neither seen nor heard from my two sisters, nor any of those who left Clarkson depot, on that memorable day.

Jacob Stroyer
Sketches of My Life in the South

PUBLICATIONS

Arlen, Michael J.
Passage to Ararat
New York: Farrar, Straus & Giroux, 1975, 293 pp; Penguin, 1982. Paper.

Account of an American author's search to find his Armenian roots. A moving personal story that contains much of interest about the Armenian tragedy and about Armenians today. SC

Bedoukian, Kerop
Some of Us Survived: The Story of an Armenian Boy
New York: Farrar, Straus & Giroux, 1979, 242 pp.

Nine-year-old curious and resourceful Kerop, his mother, the rest of his family, with the exception of his father (who had been taken away by Turkish soldiers), and thirty thousand other Armenians were evicted from their town by the Turks, gathered into a column and driven into the desert where only fifteen hundred survived. Sixty years later Kerop tells his story and that of his determined and able mother, set against the background of massacres and starvation. Read historical epilogue first. EJS

Hautzig, Esther
The Endless Steppe: Growing up in Siberia
New York: Harper & Row, 1968, 243 pp.; Scholastic. Paper.

In 1941, when the Russians occupied Vilna, the author, then 10 years old, and her family were sent to a slave labor camp in Siberia for "Capitalists — enemies of the people." Illustrates how individuals survived incredible hardships. JS

Houston, Jeanne Wakatusi and James D. Houston
Farewell to Manzanar
New York: Bantam, 1974, 160 pp. Paper.

First-person true story of a girl who was seven years old when her family was interned in a camp for Japanese Americans. Personalizes an episode in our recent American history in a way that students will find most engrossing.
JS

Rilik-Audrieux, *Toasted Bread, 1940*

Kherdian, David
The Road from Home: The Story of an Armenian Girl
New York: Greenwillow Books, 1979, 256 pp.

In 1915 the Turkish government decided to rid the country of its Armenian population. Vernon was deported with her family. The story tells of the long march by wagon and then by foot, the pain and the hardship and the death of many family members, until finally she left for America at the age of 16 as a "mail order" bride. The author is the son of Vernon, the Armenian girl. JS

Klein, Gerda Weissmann
Promise of a New Spring: the Holocaust and Renewal
Illustrations by Vincent Tarturo
Chappaqua, N.Y.; Rossel Books, 1981, 48 pp. Also paper.

A first book on the Holocaust and the meaning of survival. Based on an allegory of a forest fire, purposefully set. For the lower level elementary-school child.

Kuper, Leo
Genocide: Its Political Use in the Twentieth Century
New Haven: Yale University Press, 255 pp.

Based on the 1946 resolution of the United Nations General Assembly which recognizes genocide as "a crime under international law," the book analyzes a range of forms and cases of genocide (including a chapter on "Ther German Genocide Against the Jews") and sharply attacks the United Nations for its ineffectiveness in dealing with genocide. The book is stronger from the psychological than the legal standpoint. The first half of the book deals with the background of the U.N. Convention and with theories which might explain the phenomenon of genocide. C

Solzhenitsyn, Aleksander I.
The Gulag Archipelago 1918-1946: An Experiment in Literary Investigation
New York: Harper & Row, Parts I and II, 1974, 600 pp.; Parts III and IV, 1975, 712 pp. Also paper; Parts V, VI and VII, 1978. Also paper, 1979.

The Nobel laureate, formerly a political prisoner in the U.S.S.R., writes about the brutal dehumanizing prison camps. SC

Werfel, Franz
Forty Days of Musa Dagh
Translated from the German by Geoffrey Dunlop. New York: Carroll & Graf (Publisher's Group West), 1983, 832 pp. Paper; Amereon Ltd.

Highly recommended for readers who are not afraid of an 800-page, old-fashioned novel. An epic of the Armenian genocide, including the heroic story of an attempt by a group of Armenians to hold out on a mountaintop against the Turks. SC

Wytwycky, Bohdan
The Other Holocaust: Many Circles of Hell
Washington, DC: The Novak Report. 1980, 96pp. Paper.

A brief account of other victims of Nazism — Gypsies, Poles, etc., which does not diminish the fact that "those who were condemned to the most desperate circles in the Nazi hell were undeniably the Jews." The author ends with a plea for all to "work towards extinguishing all seeds of irrational animosity." There are some who will object to the use of the term Holocaust for these victims of Nazism. There is also some question regarding the number of victims the author refers to. Much investigative work remains to be done in this area. SC

AUDIO VISUAL

The Armenian Case
43 minutes/color/Atlantis Films

Survivors of Turkish atrocities and European and American eyewitnesses recall the chilling historical events that were to shape the destiny of the Armenian people. The film includes documentary sequences on World War I, President Woodrow Wilson, and the establishment of the Republic of Armenia and Soviet Armenia. Narrated by Mike Connors. JSC.
28 minute version: *The Forgotten Genocide*

The Memory of Justice
278 minutes/color, with black-and-white footage/ Films Incorporated

A piercing look at the Nuremberg trials and their relevance to such modern-day atrocities as My Lai. By Marcel Ophuls. SC

Relocation of Japanese Americans
2 filmstrips/black-and-white with cassettes; teacher's guide/Zenger Productions

The first filmstrip gives the historical background of the relocation of the Japanese Americans during World War II, and the second deals with the actual wartime evacuation. Throughout the presentation, the viewer is urged to decide, on the basis of given circumstances, whether the relocation was justified. JS

The Jews

If the statistics are right, the Jews constitute but one percent of the human race. It suggests a nebulous dim puff of star dust lost in the blaze of the Milky Way. Properly the Jew ought hardly to be heard of; but he is heard of, has always been heard of ... He has made a marvelous fight in this world, in all the ages; and he has done it with his hands tied behind his back.

Mark Twain
Concerning the Jews

PUBLICATIONS

Ausubel, Nathan
The Book of Jewish Knowledge
New York: Crown, 1964, 560 pp.

A single-volume guide to basic information about Jews and Judaism. Profusely illustrated. Thematic approach. JS

Bridger, David, editor
The New Jewish Encyclopedia
New York: Behrman House, 1976, 541 pp.

Excellent for student use and class libraries, especially in lower grades. Illustrated. EJS

Karel Fleischman, *Schleusen Hospital, 1942*

Fast, Howard
The Jews: Story of a People
New York: Dell, 1978, 384 pp. Paper.

The author is not a scholar but a novelist deeply involved with the subject. Traces the history of the Jews from their nomadic life in ancient Israel to the Nazi Holocaust and its aftermath. Well written. EJS

Roth, Cecil and Geoffrey Wigoder, editors
The Concise Jewish Encyclopedia
New York: Doubleday, 1980, 1,978 pp. Paper.

Although comprehensive in scope, this work emphasizes recent Jewish history and scholarship. Handy, concise. If a school library cannot afford the *Encyclopedia Judaica*, it should at least have this one volume work. Illustrated. JSC

Roth, Cecil and Geoffrey Wigoder, editors-in-chief
Encyclopedia Judaica
New York: Macmillan, 1972. 16 vols. Over 26,000 pp.

The major reference work on Jewish history, culture, religion and people in the English language. Contains syntheses of research in the various fields, plus original work by some major scholars (G. Scholem, H.L. Ginzberg). Annual supplements. Profusely illustrated, including color shots. JSC

Sachar, Howard Morley
The Course of Modern Jewish History
Updated and expanded edition. New York: Dell, 1977, 669 pp. Paper.

A history of the Jews from the French Revolution to the present. Excellent one-volume survey that synthesizes and places in perspective for the general reader the basic information accumulated by modern scholarship. Bibliography. SC

Schwarz, Leo, editor
Memoirs of My People
New York: Holt, Rinehart & Winston, 1943, 597 pp.

Excerpts from diaries and autobiographies written by Jews throughout history. JSC

Schwarz, Leo, editor
The Jewish Caravan: Great Stories of Twenty-Five Centuries
Revised and Enlarged. New York: Holt, Rinehart & Winston; Schocken, 1976, 829 pp. Paper.

Anthology of literature and fiction through the ages. Includes selections from Kafka, Buber, Stefan Zweig, as well as Biblical, Medieval and Hasidic literature. JSC.

Schweitzer, Frederick M.
A History of the Jews Since the First Century A.D.
New York: Macmillan, 1971, 319 pp. Also paper.

Set in the framework of general history, with special emphasis on the contemporary implications of Jewish history. Brief, well-written survey by a Christian scholar. JSC

Prejudice and Anti-Semitism

Prejudice is an attitude in a closed mind.

Gordon W. Allport
Psychologist

I am an anti-Semite of a much older vintage than you! I could be your father.

Xavier Vallat
Vichy's Commissioner for
Jewish Affairs, to an SS
Representative

... in her rejection of every persecution against any man, the Church, mindful of the patrimony she shares with the Jews and moved not by political reasons but by the Gospel's spiritual love, decries hatred, persecutions, displays of anti-Semitism, directed against Jews at any time and by anyone.

Second Vatican Council's
Declaration on the Relation of
the Church to Non-Christian
Religions, (October 28, 1965)

PUBLICATIONS

Allport, Gordon W.
ABC's of Scapegoating
Seventh revised edition.
New York: ADL, 1969, 36 pp.
Paper.

Briefly examines "scapegoating," sources of race prejudice in the child, types of scapegoaters, the victim, and forms of scapegoating. The theme of this pamphlet was later expanded into *The Nature of Prejudice.* JS

Allport, Gordon W.
The Nature of Prejudice
Special edition
Reading, MA: Addison-Wesley,
1979, 496 pp. Paper. (ADL)

Comprehensive and detailed
account of the phenomenon of prejudice; its roots in psychology, history and social structure; its many
varieties and expressions in inter-
personal relations and in society —
and how it can be reduced. For
teachers — and, in small doses —
for students. SC

Cohn, Norman
**Warrant for Genocide: The Myth
of the Jewish World Conspiracy
and the Protocols of the Elders
of Zion**
Chico, CA: Scholars Press, 1981,
303 pp. Paper. (ADL)

Traces how the myth of a Jewish
world conspiracy developed out of
traditional demonology after the
French Revolution, inspiring a whole
series of forgeries which culminated
in the notorious Protocols; how the
Protocols were used to justify the
massacre of Jews during the Russian civil war; how they swept the
world after World War I; how they
took possession of Hitler's mind
and became the ideology of his
most fanatical followers at home
and abroad — and helped prepare
the way for the near-extermination
of European Jewry. C

Flannery, Edward
**The Anguish of the Jews:
Twenty-Three Centuries of Anti-
Semitism**
New York: Macmillan, 1972. 332
pp. Revised 1985, Paulist Press.
Also paper. (ADL)

A concise history, country by country, century by century, by a
Catholic priest. "The pages Jews
have memorized have been torn
from our histories of the Christian
era. In a sense, this book is a rein-
sertion of these pages." SC

*Gabelko, Nina Hersch and John U.
Michaelis*
**Reducing Adolescent Prejudice:
A Handbook**
New York: Teachers College Press,
1981, 226 pp. Also paper. (ADL)

Stimulating and practical interdisciplinary approach that can be
implemented in courses in U.S. and
world history, government, sociology, psychology and economics.
Includes readings for students and
moral dilemma cases. Teacher.

Katz, Jacob
**From Prejudice to Destruction:
Anti-Semitism, 1700-1933**
Cambridge: Harvard University
Press, 1980, 398 pp. Also paper,
1982, 400 pp.

A major reinterpretation of modern
anti-Semitism by a leading Jewish
social historian. The author rejects

the scapegoat theory and revises the prevalent thesis that medieval and modern forms of animosity against Jews are fundamentally different. Stating that "the anti-Semitic movement of the 19th century which culminated in the Nazi period stands revealed as the product of the peculiar constellation of historical circumstance," he cautions: "The attempt to foresee the future on the basis of its analogies with the past is a futile undertaking. What the historian can do ... is to assess the extent to which the elements involved in a past constellation of events are still operative in the present and how reactions to its consequences seem to shape up — without pretending to know what new combinations may emerge out of these and other unapprehended elements."
C

Mosse, George L.
Germans and Jews: The Right, the Left, and the Search for a "Third Force" in Pre-Nazi Germany
New York: Howard Fertig, 1970, 260 pp.

A collection of essays that probes the intellectual roots of German totalitarianism, with special emphasis on the role of anti-Semitism and the position of the German Jews.
C.

Quinley, Harold E. and Charles Y. Glock
Anti-Semitism in America
New York: The Free Press, 1979, 257 pp,; Transaction Books, 1983, 259 pp. Paper. (ADL)

A review of research findings from scores of studies on prejudice and anti-Semitism, including the nine conducted by the ADL and the University of California Research Center over a number of years, as part of the "Patterns of American Prejudice" series. One of the sections focuses on the causes for and the extent of anti-Semitism among the young. Surveys indicate that anti-Semitism is nurtured among youths who have not developed the "cognitive skills and sophistication to combat it." In addition, it is discovered that anti-Semitic beliefs in children are more prevalent when Jews are present in a school population than when they are not. Determines that anti-Semitism remains a "significant feature of adolescent life." C

Sartre, Jean-Paul
Anti-Semite and Jew
Translated from the French by George J. Becker.
New York: Schocken, 1965, 153 pp. Paper.

Psychological analysis of the marginal Jew and the anti-Semite. Originally published in 1946. Most readable. JSC

Shiman, David A.
The Prejudice Book: Activities for the Classroom
New York: ADL, 1981, 176 pp. Paper.

Thirty-seven activities dealing with perceptions and feelings about one's self and others, generalizations and stereotypes, prejudice and discrimination. While intended for 9-to 13-year-olds, much of it can be used with older students, as well. Includes a Teacher Self-Examination Questionnaire. Teacher.

AUDIO-VISUAL

Eye of the Storm
25 minutes/color/not cleared for TV/ADL

In this ABC-TV News special, the effects of prejudice are made patently clear as cameras record a unique two-day experiment conducted by a third-grade teacher in a Midwest agricultural community. On the first day, the teacher separated her class into "superior" and "inferior" groups, based solely on eye color. Blue-eyed children were "superior," brown-eyed children "inferior." On the second day the roles were reversed. Attitudes, behavior and classroom performance changed as children suffered segregation, discrimination, and the devastating virus of prejudice. JS

Understanding Prejudice
3 filmstrips with cassettes/teacher's guide/ADL

This three-part color-sound series examines the components and workings of prejudice, how it develops and grows, how it is destructive, and how it can be eradicated. Using three main headings: (1) stereotyping, (2) the "master race" myth, (3) scapegoating, the series uses examples which relate to the adolescent student's experiences. JS

You've Got to be Taught to Hate
12 minutes/color and black-and-white/cleared for TV/ADL

An edited version of the award-winning documentary *The Victims*, this film is a primer on prejudice and the ways in which it is transmitted to children during their formative and adolescent years. Designed as a discussion stimulator, particularly for junior and senior high school, the film demonstrates that prejudice is a disease that is subtly transmitted, that it can be "caught," even without knowing it and, if "sick" with the virus, one becomes isolated from the "marvelous variety" of the world and its people. JSC

The Controlled Society

The totalitarian state tries to control the thoughts and emotions of its subjects at least as completely as it controls its actions.

George Orwell

PUBLICATIONS

Arendt, Hannah
The Origins of Totalitarianism
Magnolia, MA.: Peter Smith, 1983; Harcourt, Brace, Jovanovich, 1968. Paper. 3 vols.

Brilliant, erudite and influential analysis of the genesis and the nature of Nazi and Stalinist totalitarianism. Arendt, an eminent political theorist, shows the central importance of anti-Semitism to totalitarian ideology and of concentration camps to the organization of the totalitarian system. Takes issue with the theses of Cohn and Sartre (see section on Anti-Semitism). Harcourt Brace has published *The Origins of Totalitarianism* as three separate paperbacks: *Anti-Semitism, Imperialism,* and *Totalitarianism.* C

Butler William
Butterfly Revolution
New York: Ballantine, 1979. Paper.

Novel dealing with a youth at a boys summer camp which becomes a totalitarian operation. Good for exploring organizational techniques and psychological motivations of a totalitarian movement. May be conceptually difficult for below-average 9th- or 10th-grade students. JS

Greene, Nathanael, ed.
Fascism
Arlington Heights, IL: Harlan Davidson, 1968, 302 pp.

An anthology on the origins and definitions of Fascism: the Italian example; German Poetry, and Fascism: Spain and France. Among the contributors: Mosse, Nolte, Bullock, Mussolini. Emphasis on the substance and meaning of Fascist doctrines and the roles played by key personalities. SC

Huxley, Aldous
Brave New World
Cutchogue, NY: Buccaneer Books, 1982 reprint; Harper & Row, 1979, 177 pp. Paper

Utopian vision of the future involving centralized control. May be difficult for below-average student but can still be used. Conceptually difficult. JSC

Orwell, George
Animal Farm
New York: Harcourt, Brace, Jovanovich, 1954; Signet, 1974, 128 pp. Paper.

"All animals are equal but some are more equal than others." Allegory on an imposed "egalitarian" society. Classic. JSC

Orwell, George
1984
New York: Harcourt, Brace, Jovanovich, 1983; Signet Classic/New American Library, 1984 Commemorative edition, 268 pp. Paper.

Compelling novel about a negative Utopia and totalitarian control. May be conceptually difficult for some 9th and 10th graders, but they should be given a chance. JSC

Rubenstein, Richard
The Cunning of History: Mass Death and the American Future
New York: Harper & Row, 1975, 113 pp.

According to Rubenstein, mass death and wholesale extermination are the result of bureaucracy, technology, and the notion of "superfluous people." C

AUDIO-VISUAL

Puppets
11 minutes/black-and-white/cleared for TV/ADL

A puppet actor steps out of his role in a marionette performance of *Julius Caesar* to provide a unique lesson on totalitarianism and conformity. He serves as guide backstage and back through history, introducing the audience to infamous charlatans and despots and the victims who suffered through their treachery. He reveals how these villains, from Satan to Mussolini and Hitler, used the scapegoat technique to gain adherence from their followers. EJS.

Resources: Major Holocaust Education and Resource Centers

American Jewish Archives
3101 Clifton Avenue
Cincinnati, OH 45220
(513) 221-1875

An internationally recognized institution dedicated to the study of, and the literature about the American and Western Hemispheric Jewish experience. Repository for World Jewish Congress papers — more than 2 million pages of documentation highlighting activities of the WJC in its rescue and relief efforts during the Holocaust. Other collections reflect the response of American Jewish religious and secular organizations to the Holocaust, most notably the papers of philanthropist Felix Warburg; the papers of the Central Conference of American Rabbis and the Union of American Hebrew Congregations; and the records of the Hebrew Union College and the Jewish Institute of Religion headed by Rabbi Stephen Wise.

The Anne Frank Institute of Philadelphia
Box 2147
Philadelphia, PA 19103
(215) 667-5437

Housed at Temple University, the Institute sponsors an annual conference on Teaching the Holocaust, which attempts to reach the entire community about the importance of teaching lessons on the Holocaust and its ethical implications; and a "Tour of Remembrance" for adults to camps and former centers of Jewish life in Europe. It publishes the proceedings of its conferences and collections of bibliographies and uses. Works with the Philadelphia schools.

The International Center for Holocaust Studies, Anti-Defamation League of B'nai B'rith
823 United Nations Plaza
New York, NY 10017
(212) 490-2525

Produces and distributes films, filmstrips, publications. Primary focus is educational institutions. Conducts local, national and international staff-development programs. Consultant for community programs and school curriculums. Works through 30 regional offices in this country. Library of publications, curriculum guides and films. Publishes *Dimensions*, a journal of Holocaust studies.

The Center of Holocaust Studies/ Documentation and Research
1609 Avenue J
Brooklyn, NY 11230
(718) 338-6494

Major Oral History Project: Interviews with survivors and former American soldiers who participated in liberating the concentration camps. The tapes are transcribed, verified, and catalogued. The Center also collects documents, photostats of letters, artifacts, etc., from the period 1933-45. It has an annual lecture series, a library and a travel-

ing photographic exhibit.

Facing History and Ourselves National Foundation, Inc.
25 Kennard Road
Brookline, MA 02146
(617) 232-1595

Interdisciplinary teacher training and curriculum development workshops. Also adult educational programs and community organizations. Resource Center maintains 60 films, 30 slide tape and filmstrip kits, 150 videotapes, 100 oral tapes, 500 books and an extensive collection of posters, articles and magazines used with the program.

Friends of Le Chambon
8033 Sunset Boulevard
Suite 784
Los Angeles, CA 90064
(213) 650-1774

Asks and seeks to answer one neglected question: Why did the people of Le Chambon and others like them act decently during the Holocaust years while the rest of the world turned away? Holdings include valuable documents, photographs and other materials related to righteous conduct during the Nazi era.

Holocaust Awareness Institute
Univ. of Denver/Center for Judaic Study
Denver, CO 80208
(303) 753-2830

Community programming. Coordinates Holocaust Days of Remembrance observances in the Denver area and has numerous other programs throughout the year. Small resource library, including some survivor tapes.

Holocaust Center of Greater Pittsburgh

242 McKee Place
Pittsburgh, PA 15213
(412) 682-7111

Full service educational resource center. Library (print and audiovisual). Programs: teacher training; curriculum development; speaking engagements; exhibits; production of education materials; community wide programs with other organizations; annual Holocaust remembrance programs; writing contest; consultations.

The Holocaust Library and Research Center of San Francisco

601 14 Avenue
San Francisco, CA 94118
(415) 751-6040

Subcommittee of the Committee of Remembrance of the JCR, San Francisco, Marin Peninsula, in cooperation with the Bureau of Jewish Education Community Library. Library, some documents and an exhibit. It is soliciting more documentation and the names of survivors and refugees in order to compile a directory.

Holocaust Memorial Center

6602 West Maple Road
West Bloomfield, MI 48033
(313) 661-0840

Library and Archives concentrates on: documentation and literature of the Holocaust; destroyed communities of Europe; Jewish life and culture in prewar Europe; Jewish-Christian relations in historical perspective.

Holocaust Survivors Memorial Foundation

350 Fifth Avenue
Suite 3508
New York, NY 10118
(212) 594-8765

Devoted exclusively to the funding of Holocaust-related projects. Supports: Institute for Holocaust Studies at the Graduate Center of the City University of New York; survivor and oral history conferences and other special events; grants to researchers, playwrights, filmmakers, writers, preservations projects and oral history projects. Supports Holocaust courses.

The Jack P. Eisner Institute For Holocaust Studies

of the Graduate School and University Center of The City University of New York
33 West 42nd Street
New York, NY 10036
(212) 790-4517

Sponsors free seminars and lectures, including annual series of 10 community lectures. Sponsors international conferences. Free in-service course on teaching about the Holocaust offered to primary and secondary school teachers. Counsels students interested in Holocaust studies.

Leo Baeck Institute
129 East 73rd Street
New York, NY 10021
(212) RH4-6400

Although not dealing exclusively or primarily with the Holocaust, the fact that it is an institute devoted to German Jewish life inevitably makes the Holocaust a significant part of its work. A serious research and archival center. Monthly lecture series. Publications include Yearbook and newsletter.

Memorial Center for Holocaust Studies
7900 Northhaven Road
Dallas, TX 75230
(214) 750-4654

Memorial center includes memorabilia, weapons, camp uniforms, passports, yellow arm bands, barbed wire and other artifacts. Study center has over one thousand volume library pertaining to anti-Semitism and the Holocaust as well as rare and out-of-print publications and magazines. Programs include guided tours, in-service teacher training and video taping of survivor testimonies.

The Montreal Holocaust Memorial Centre of the Jewish Public Library
5151 Cote St. Catherine Road
Montreal H3W IM6, Canada
(514) 735-2386

Collection of documents, photographs, artifacts, ranging from the end of the 19th century to post-World War II. Permanent and annual exhibits, memorial room. Educational programs (elementary school to university, and community organizations) in English, French, and Yiddish.

National Archives and Records Administration
8th & Pennsylvania Avenue NW
Washington, DC 20408
(202) 523-3340

Captured German records. War crimes trial records. Records of U.S. Government agencies documenting war crimes and genocide in Europe and North Africa from 1933 to 1945, as well as attempts at rescue, failures to rescue, and liberation of survivors. Records are mainly textual, much of it in microfilm, but also includes substantial amounts of audiovisual materials. Finding aids are available. available.

National Jewish Conference Center
421 7th Avenue, 4th Fl.
New York, NY 10001
(212) 714-9500

Conducts periodic faculty seminars. Sponsored the "First International Conference on Children of Holocaust Survivors;" its major focus was mental health.

New York City Holocaust Memorial Commission
111 West 40th Street
3rd Floor
New York, N.Y. 10018
(212) 221-1573

Working to establish a museum, library, archival center and lecture facility as a memorial to the victims of the Holocaust. Three themes: Jewish immigration experience in New York; European Jewish life prior to the Holocaust; Rise of Nazism and the Holocaust. (Target opening date: 1987.)

New York State Museum Holocaust Center/Exhibit
New York State Cultural Education Center
Albany, N.Y. 12230
(518) 474-5801

Permanent Exhibit Area: History of the Holocaust; US inaction; "temporary haven" for 982 Refugees in Oswego, N.Y. and the positive actions of the inhabitants of this small upstate community.

Simon Wiesenthal Center of Holocaust Studies
9769 West Pico Blvd.
Los Angeles, CA 90035
(213) 553-9036

Library, archives and permanent exhibit. Plans for research center. Plan to create master list of survivors in U.S. "Outreach" program to schools, also bring classes into the center.

St. Louis Center for Holocaust Studies
12 Millstone Campus Drive
St. Louis MO 63146
(314) 432-0020

Founded by the Jewish Federation. It has community lecture series, commemorative programs, art exhibits, book and film library. Planning to work with schools, public and parochial, within the area.

United States Holocaust Memorial Council
2000 L Street NW
Washington, DC 20036
(202) 653-9152

U.S. Government-sponsored Holocaust institution, established by a unanimous vote of Congress. The President of the United States appoints 55 Council members; 10 are members of Congress. Conducts annual national civic commemoration of Days of Remembrance in Washington D.C. and encourages civic commemorations in state capitals and cities. Annual Evening of Commemoration through the Performing Arts. Conducts international conferences. Past meetings: Liberators Conference (1981); Faith in Humankind: Rescuers of Jews during the Holocaust (1984). Provides materials, including *Directory of Holocaust Resource Centers in North America.*

Video Archive for Holocaust Testimonies at Yale

Sterling Memorial Library Yale Univ.
New Haven, CT 06520
(203) 436-2157

Records and preserves for educational use video taped testimony of survivors - and other witnesses of the Nazi persecutions. Workshops in video-interviewing offered nationally. Depository for all videotaped testimonies made by affiliates in the U.S. and other countries. Indexes of all testimonies and viewing facilities for appropriate research and educational purposes. Records in the Research Libraries Information Network (RLIN) on-line data base, a national information retrieval system. Sponsors annual conference to coordinate activites in this area.

Witness to the Holocaust Project

Emory University
Atlanta, GA 30322
(404) 329-7525

Focuses on recording the testimony of persons who witnessed the camps during the liberation period — military personnel, relief agency workers, press corps.

YIVO Institute for Jewish Research

1048 Fifth Avenue
New York, NY 10028
(212) 535-6700

YIVO does not deal exclusively with the Holocaust, but it has probably the finest library on the Holocaust in this country as well as what is certainly the greatest photographic collection. Its staff includes scholars and researchers. Publishes an Annual YIVO *Bulletin*; photos and slides for purchase and/or rental. The Max Weinreich Graduate Center (YIVO) includes courses that deal with aspects of the Holocaust.

Other Resource Centers, Libraries, Archives, and Collections

American Federation of Jewish Fighters, Camp Inmates, and Nazi Victims
505 Fifth Avenue, 12th Floor
New York, NY 10017

American Jewish Historical Society
Brandeis University
2 Thornton Road
Waltham, MA 02154

Baltimore Jewish Council
101 West Mount Royal Avenue
Baltimore, MD 21201

Cincinnati Interfaith Holocaust Foundation
2615 Clifton Avenue
Cincinnati, OH 45220

Holocaust Center of the North Shore Jewish Federation
4 Community Road
Marblehead, MA 01945

Holocaust Memorial Foundation of Illinois
P.O. Box 574
Northbrook, IL 60022

Holocaust Remembrance Committee
Toronto Jewish Congress
16 Pinewood Avenue
Toronto, Ontario M6C 2V1, Canada

Holocaust Resource & Educational Center, Federation of Greater Orlando
851 Maitland Avenue
Maitland, FL 32751

Holocaust Resource Center of Buffalo
2640 North Forest Road
Getzville, NY 14068

Hoover Institution on War, Revolution, and Peace
Stanford University
Stanford, CA 94305

Institute for Research In History
432 Park Avenue South
New York, NY 10016

Institute for the Study of Genocide
444 West 56th Street
New York, NY 10019

International Network of Children of Jewish Holocaust Survivors
1 Park Avenue
New York, NY 10016

The Jewish Museum
1109 Fifth Avenue
New York, NY 10028

Jewish Theological Seminary
3080 Broadway
New York, NY 10027

Life Center for Holocaust Studies
844 Central Avenue
Woodmere, NY 11598

Martyrs Memorial and Museum, Federation of Greater Los Angeles
6505 Wilshire Blvd.
Los Angeles, CA 90048

National Center for Jewish Film
Lown Building 102
Brandeis University
Waltham, MA 02154

National Holocaust Remembrance Committee
Canadian Jewish Congress
1590 Avenue Dr. Penfield
Montreal, Quebec H3G 1C5, Canada

Queensborough Community College-Oral History Project
56th Avenue & Springfield Blvd.
Bayside, NY 11364

Resource Center for Holocaust and Genocide Studies
Library Room L403
505 Ramapo Valley Road
Mahwah, NJ 07430

Southeast Florida Holocaust Memorial Center
Florida International University
NW 151 Street & Biscayne Blvd.
North Miami, FL 33181

State Historical Society of Wisconsin
816 State Street
Madison, WI 53706

The Tauber Institute
Brandeis University
Waltham, MA 02154

Warsaw Ghetto Resistance Organization
122 West 30th Street
New York, NY 10001

AUDIO-VISUAL
DISTRIBUTORS

Alden
7820 Twentieth Avenue
Brooklyn, NY 11214

Allied Artists
15 Columbus Circle
New York, NY 10023

Almi-Cinema Five
1585 Broadway
New York, NY 10036

**American Federation of Jewish
Fighters, Camp Inmates, and
Nazi Victims**
505 5th Avenue, 12th Floor
New York, NY 10017

**Anti-Defamation League of B'nai
B'rith (ADL)**
823 U.N. Plaza
New York, NY 10017

Atlantis Films
1252 La Granda Dr.
Thousand Oaks, CA 91362

Audio Visual Narrative Arts
Box 9
Pleasantville, NY 10570

Blackwood Productions
251 W. 57th Street
New York, NY 10019

Documentary Photo Aids
P.O. Box 956
Mt. Dora, FL 32757

Educational Activity Aids
P.O. Box 392
Freeport, NY 11520

Educational Audio-Visual
19 Marble Avenue
Pleasantville, NY 10570

Films Incorporated
733 Green Bay Road
Wilmette, IL 60091

Icarus
200 Park Avenue, So.
New York, NY 10003

Center for Humanities
90 S. Bedford Road
Mt. Kisco, NY 10549

Cinema Guild
1697 Broadway, Suite 802
New York, NY 10019

Columbia Pictures
711 5th Avenue
New York, NY 10022

Direct Cinema, Ltd.
P.O. Box 69589
Los Angeles, CA 90069

Images
300 Phillip Park Road
Mamaroneck, NY 10543

Jewish Labor Committee
25 East 21st Street
New York, NY 10010

Jewish Lecture Bureau
15 E. 26th Street
New York, NY 10010

MGM/United Artists
729 7th Avenue
New York, NY 10019

Multimedia
140 W. 9th Street
Cincinnati, OH 45202

**National Academy of Adult
Jewish Studies**
155 5th Avenue
New York, NY 10010

Phoenix Films/BFA
470 Park Avenue, So.
New York, NY 10016

Production Form Company
Box 147
214 W. 8th Street
Logan, IA 51546

Scholastic International
50 West 44th Street
New York, NY 10036

**Simon & Schuster
Communications**
1230 Avenue of the Americas
New York, NY 10020

Social Studies School Service
10000 Culver Blvd.
Culver City, CA 90232

Swank
201 S. Jefferson Avenue
St. Louis, MO 63103

Texture Films
P.O. Box 1337
Skokie, IL 60076

Zenger Productions
P.O. Box 802
Culver City, CA 90232

Index

Publications Index

Author Index

Audio-Visual Index